Mob Chronicles

Mob Chronicles

Anton Schwartz

© 2025 Anton Schwartz

hello.antschwartz@gmail.com
Edition: BoD · Books on Demand, 31 avenue Saint-Rémy,
57600 Forbach, bod@bod.fr
Print: Libri Plureos GmbH, Friedensallee 273,
22763 Hamburg (Allemagne)

ISBN: 978-2-8106-2603-8
Legal deposit: : Février 2025

"The Mafia is no fairy tale. It is ominously real, and it has scarred the face of America with almost every conceivable type of criminal violence."

Estes Kefauver
Chairman of the Senate Committee on Organized Crime

CONTENT

FOREWORD	2
MUGSHOTS	6
ELEGANCE	18
CRIME	30
DOLLARS	42
JUSTICE	52
ODDITIES	66
HEALTH	80
BEHIND BARS	90
HIGH STAKES	98
SWING TIME	108
HOLLYWOOD & FICTION	120
BAGATELLE	130
BUON APPETITO	136
BIBLIOGRAPHY	146
SOURCES	156

Just like the conquest of the West, the Civil War, or the revolutions of Silicon Valley, the mafia is a fundamental part of the extraordinary history of the United States. Rising to prominence in the early 1920s with Prohibition, organized crime gradually infiltrated every vein of society and eventually impacted the commerce and politics of the entire nation. Figures such as Al Capone, Lucky Luciano, and Meyer Lansky became some of the infamous legends that emerged from speakeasies, ultimately forging a myth of power and wealth in the eyes of several generations of Americans.

Despite the murders, violence, and sometimes sordid lives faced by members of the underworld, Hollywood and classic books like *The Godfather* elevated these tuxedoed criminals to the status of glamorous icons, seemingly governed by honor and family. The reality, however, was far darker. Behind the allure of these clandestine empires lay gangsters, swindlers, and sometimes traitors, ready to sell out their former associates to avoid spending their lives in prison. Of course, this somber side is offset by the brilliance of individuals who rose from grimy alleyways to the heights of society, propelled by their defiance of the law and their extraordinary instincts.

Countless books on organized crime have already been published, and any new word on the subject might seem redundant. Yet, while the mafia has entered collective memory, the personal stories of those who shaped it remain largely unknown. Did you know Joseph Bonanno took acting classes before leading one of New York's most powerful families? Or that Al Capone formed a banjo band while imprisoned at Alcatraz? Has anyone told you how Santo Trafficante Jr., Florida's crime boss, narrowly escaped the brutal prisons of Castro's Cuba? All these life fragments are an invaluable treasure for better understanding the thousands of souls who built one of the most extraordinary criminal organizations this nation has ever seen.

Thanks to research based on first-rate sources—such as CIA archives, period newspapers, FBI files, court reports, and the works of numerous credible authors—you will find here two hundred anecdotes, each more astonishing than the last, meticulously annotated and classified into twelve thematic chapters.

Smell the fumes of bootleg bourbon. Listen to that muffled jazz. Step into a secret world, where the rain of the *Roaring Twenties* washes away the sins of the night.

MUGSHOTS

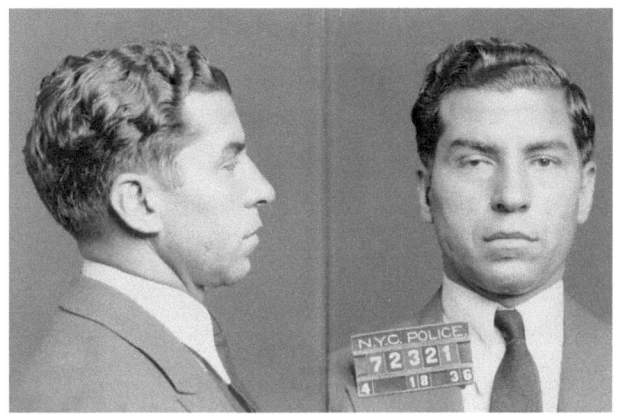

Mugshot of Lucky Luciano in 1931

More than one hundred and forty mafia-related figures are mentioned in this book. Although their roles are regularly recalled throughout the anecdotes, here is nonetheless for your convenience a gallery of the main individuals who have shaped the history of organized crime in America.

AL CAPONE | (1899-1947)

The iconic boss of Chicago's Outfit. He made a fortune during Prohibition and earned the title of "Public Enemy Number One" through ruthless violence to expand his power.

ALBERT ANASTASIA | (1902-1957)

A close associate of Luciano, known as the "Lord High Executioner." He led the notorious contract killing organization called "Murder Inc."

ALPHONSE "LITTLE AL" D'ARCO | (1932-2019)

Acting boss of the Lucchese family. He was the first leader of one of New York's Five Families to testify as a government witness.

ANTHONY "GASPIPE" CASSO | (1942-2020)

Underboss of the Lucchese family. Allegedly responsible for over thirty murders, he was expelled from the witness protection program after multiple violations.

ARNOLD ROTHSTEIN | (1882-1928)

A wealthy gangster, professional gambler, and financier of the mafia. He made a fortune during Prohibition and worked closely with Luciano and Meyer Lansky.

BENJAMIN "BUGSY" SIEGEL | (1906-1947)

A friend of Meyer Lansky and Hollywood stars, he played a leading role in the development of Las Vegas, notably by creating the famous *Flamingo* hotel-casino.

CARLO GAMBINO | (1902-1976)

Boss of the Gambino family. He was one of the most powerful leaders of the American underworld. Despite five decades of crime, he served only twenty-two months in prison.

CARMINE GALANTE | (1910-1979)

Unofficial boss of the Bonanno family. Rarely seen without his cigar, he masterminded a massive drug trafficking operation between Canada and the United States.

CHARLES "LUCKY" LUCIANO | (1897-1962)

Boss of the Luciano family. One of the most powerful figures in mafia history, he is widely regarded as the founder of modern organized crime.

"CRAZY" JOE GALLO | (1929-1972)

A lieutenant in the Colombo family. Frustrated with the greed of his boss, Joe Profaci, he sparked a deadly war by kidnapping four high-ranking members of the organization.

DUTCH SCHULTZ | (1901-1935)

A New York gang leader. He made a considerable fortune during Prohibition but was executed by Luciano due to his volatile and unpredictable nature.

ENOCH "NUCKY" JOHNSON | (1883-1968)

Treasurer of Atlantic City. He refused to enforce Prohibition in his city and forged close ties with organized crime. His life inspired the television series *Boardwalk Empire*.

FRANK COSTELLO | (1891-1973)

Boss of the Luciano family. Nicknamed the "Prime Minister," he moved effortlessly between the criminal underworld and the polished world of politics, wielding immense power.

FRANK SINATRA | (1915-1998)

An internationally renowned jazz singer. Despite selling over one hundred and fifty million records and achieving iconic status, his image suffered from shady connections with certain gangsters.

GEORGES REMUS | (1901-1935)

A lawyer and pharmacist. He exploited a legal loophole in the Prohibition Act, becoming one of the mafia's most significant suppliers of alcohol.

GREGORY SCARPA SR. | (1928-1994)

 A lieutenant in the Colombo family and an FBI informant for thirty years. Nicknamed "The Grim Reaper," he was notorious for his brutality.

J. EDGAR HOOVER | (1895-1972)

 The legendary director of the FBI for thirty-seven years. He outlasted eight presidents and maintained compromising files on numerous prominent figures.

JAMES "WHITEY" BULGER | (1929-2018)

 Boss of Boston's Winter Hill Gang. He evaded capture for sixteen years, becoming the United States' most wanted fugitive after Osama bin Laden.

JOE "THE BOSS" MASSERIA | (1886-1931)

 Boss of New York's mafia in the 1920s. He started a deadly war against his rival Salvatore Maranzano and was assassinated by Luciano.

JOE PROFACI | (1897-1962)

Boss of the Profaci family. He ruled his crew with an iron fist for over thirty years. Deeply religious, he was also one of the country's largest importers of olive oil.

JOEY MASSINO | (1943-2023)

Boss of the Bonanno family. He brought his criminal organization back into prominence after it was decimated by the FBI's "Donnie Brasco" operation.

JOHN GOTTI | (1940-2002)

Boss of the Gambino family. He rose to power by orchestrating the murder of his boss, Paul Castellano, and became infamous for his sharp suits and numerous courtroom acquittals.

JOSEPH BONANNO | (1905-2002)

Boss of the Bonanno family. He played a key role in the formation of New York's Five Families and broke the omerta by publishing his autobiography.

JOSEPH D. PISTONE | (1939)

An FBI agent who infiltrated the Bonanno family from 1976 to 1981 under the alias "Donnie Brasco." His high-risk operation led to the indictment of two hundred gangsters.

MARIO PUZO | (1920-1999)

An author and screenwriter specializing in crime stories. He rose to fame with the publication of his seminal novel, *The Godfather*.

MEYER LANSKY | (1902-1983)

An associate of Luciano. Known for his sharp intellect, he played a crucial role in expanding the mafia's influence in Cuba, Las Vegas, and New York.

MICKEY COHEN | (1913-1976)

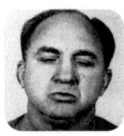
Boss of the Cohen family. After working under Al Capone and later Benjamin Siegel, he established his own criminal enterprises in Los Angeles.

PAUL CASTELLANO | (1915-1985)

Boss of the Gambino family. He succeeded the legendary Carlo Gambino but was assassinated by John Gotti, who resented, among other things, his excessive greed.

PAUL VARIO | (1914-1988)

A lieutenant in the Lucchese family operating in Brooklyn. He was portrayed as the character Paul Cicero in Martin Scorsese's film *Goodfellas*.

SALVATORE MARANZANO | (1886-1931)

A rival of Joe "The Boss" Masseria. He declared himself the supreme leader of New York's mafia in 1931, only to be betrayed and murdered by Luciano a few months later.

SAM GIANCANA | (1908-1975)

Boss of Chicago's Outfit. He was involved in John F. Kennedy's election and a CIA plot to assassinate Fidel Castro.

SANTO TRAFFICANTE JR. | (1914-1987)

Boss of the Trafficante family. He controlled much of Florida's underworld and expanded his criminal operations into Cuba.

TOMMY LUCCHESE | (1897-1962)

Boss of the Lucchese family. Highly respected by his peers, he mentored Santo Trafficante Jr., who would later become Florida's top mob boss.

VINCENT "THE CHIN" GIGANTE | (1928-2005)

Boss of the Genovese family. Extremely cautious, he threatened death to anyone who uttered his name and feigned insanity to avoid law enforcement scrutiny.

VINCENZO "BIG JIM" COLOSIMO | (1878-1920)

The first boss of Chicago's Outfit. He unified the city's numerous gangs and built a criminal empire based on prostitution, later taken over by Johnny Torrio and Al Capone.

.

VITO GENOVESE | (1914-1988)

A major figure in organized crime, he succeeded Frank Costello as head of the Luciano family, renaming it after himself. He was also an ally of Italian dictator Benito Mussolini.

ELEGANCE

Meyer Lansky posing for the World Telegram

Paul Castellano, boss of the Gambino family, ordered the execution of his daughter's boyfriend after learning the young man had physically compared him to Frank Perdue, a bald businessman known for his chicken empire[1]. The joker's body was never found[2].

The gangster Benjamin "Bugsy" Siegel was terrified at the thought of losing his hair. He loved slicking it back but bitterly noticed that his once-thick hair was gradually thinning. Determined to stop his early-stage baldness, he tried in vain all kinds of anti-hair-loss lotions[3]. No one dared upset him on this highly sensitive topic. The barbers at the *Gornik-Drucker* salon in Beverly Hills diplomatically reassured him that they could see new growth appearing here and there on his scalp, and his friends took turns lying to him without hesitation. But all these efforts failed to comfort Siegel, who even turned to witchcraft to ward off baldness. One evening, he obtained a lock of actor George Raft's hair, placed it in an envelope along with $2,500 in small bills, and threw it into his fireplace[4].

———

After being on the run for sixteen long years[5], James "Whitey" Bulger, the Boston mafia boss, was identified by Anna Björnsdóttir, a former Miss Iceland and participant in Miss Universe, who lived in his neighborhood in Santa Monica[6]. After seeing the criminal's photo on CNN[7], she realized that her neighbor was none other than the country's most wanted fugitive, second only to Osama bin Laden[8]. The beauty queen earned two million dollars for assisting law enforcement[9].

———

Al Capone earned the nickname "Scarface" from the three scars that streaked his face[10]. The largest ran ten centimeters, from the top of his left jaw to the bottom of his lips[11]. These disfiguring marks appeared when he was eighteen[12], while working as a bartender at the *Harvard Inn* on Coney Island[13]. Smitten with a female patron, the gangster whispered in her ear that she had "a nice ass." Unfortunately, her brother, Frank Galluccio, overheard the inappropriate comment and slashed Capone's face with a knife[14]. Self-conscious about his injuries, Capone applied thick layers of talcum powder to his cheek and only presented his unscathed right profile to photographers[15]. He even claimed his scars were from shrapnel wounds sustained in France during World War I, though he never set foot on a battlefield[16]. Due to a veto from the powerful Joe "The Boss" Masseria, Capone was never able to take revenge on Galluccio. However, he eventually admitted his wrongdoing and frequently hired his attacker as a bodyguard during trips to New York[17].

In 1944, Frank Costello forgot $27,000 in a taxi. The money was seized by law enforcement and held until its legality could be proven. Against the advice of his lawyer, who urged him to keep a low profile, the boss of the Luciano family decided—out of vanity—to sue the New York police[18] and present himself in the best possible light to the jury to reclaim his money. Costello began meticulously perfecting his appearance, indulging in multiple tanning lamp sessions to refine his complexion and refusing to wear a cheap suit. In the end, Costello won the case. However, after taxes and legal fees were deducted, he was left with only $120 in his pocket[19].

———

Samuzzo "Samoots" Amatuna, a Chicago gangster, owned two hundred silk shirts in his wardrobe. One day, a traveling laundryman accidentally burned one of his prized garments. Driven into a frenzy by the news, Amatuna chased the man through the city streets and shot his horse in retaliation[20].

———

Albert Anastasia, leader of the infamous hit squad "Murder Inc.," was killed while getting a haircut at the *Park Sheraton Hotel* in New York. After taking four bullets to the body, the "High Lord Executioner" managed to get up but mistakenly attacked the reflection of his two killers in the salon mirror. His error was swiftly punished with a final shot to the head, ending his life[21]. Anastasia's chair is now on display at the *Mob Museum* in Las Vegas[22].

———

The mobster Joseph Doto called himself Joe Adonis, after the Greek god Adonis, who was passionately loved by the goddess Aphrodite. Like his namesake, Doto enjoyed admiring his own beauty in mirrors. One day, while he was combing his hair, Luciano quipped, "Who do you think you are, Rudolph Valentino?" to which Doto replied that, "For looks, that guy's a bum."[23]

Vincenzo "Big Jim" Colosimo, the first boss of Chicago's Outfit, was passionate about diamonds. He wore them on every finger and sported a horseshoe adorned with precious stones on his vest. His belt buckles and suspenders were also encrusted with glittering gems. Thanks to his work as a fence for stolen jewelry, he was able to acquire opals and rubies at very favorable prices. The rare diamonds he didn't wear were carefully stored in his pockets, ready to be gifted to the police officers under his thumb[24].

Enoch "Nucky" Johnson, the unofficial boss of Atlantic City, placed great importance on his appearance. Every morning, his valet, Louis Kessel, selected one of his hundred custom-tailored suits and adorned it with a red carnation for the perfect touch. In the summer, Johnson favored lavender and chocolate-colored jackets. And when winter's icy winds swept the Atlantic coast, he donned a raccoon fur coat[25]. His ensemble was completed with spats, leather shoes, and a cane, embodying the perfect gentleman. During the day, Johnson particularly enjoyed strolling along the boardwalk, handing out a few dollars to passersby. When he wasn't walking, Kessel chauffeured him to his appointments in a stunning blue Rolls-Royce[26]. Nicknamed the "Czar of the Ritz" due to his residence in a suite at the *Ritz-Carlton Hotel*[27], Johnson also owned a Cadillac, a Lincoln, and a Ford, which he used depending on his mood[28].

Salvatore Maranzano, boss of the future Bonanno family, spoke twelve languages and was passionate about Julius Caesar's military campaigns[29]. In a twist of irony, he died from multiple stab wounds, just like his hero[30].

Arnold Rothstein, the mafia's financier, hated his teeth, considering them uneven and not white enough. He thus asked a dentist to replace them and underwent an eight-hour surgery. At nightfall, he then left the office to collect money from his many debtors, as if nothing had happened[31].

Frank "Bumpy" Lucas, the African-American crime boss of Harlem, wrote poetry and played chess. Defying the racist prejudices of his time, he even dated a white woman who worked as a columnist for *Vanity Fair* magazine[32].

The media had a certain fascination with John Gotti, boss of the Gambino family[33]. In stark contrast to the discretion typically advocated by mafia family leaders, Gotti embraced a public image of a Hollywood-style gangster[34], showcasing a refined fashion sense that earned him the nickname "Dapper Don."[35] Even the highly respected *Time* magazine joined in on the frenzy, commissioning pop art icon Andy Warhol[36] to illustrate the cover of its September 29, 1986, issue[37]. Frustrated by the endless press coverage, Jules J. Bonavolonta, head of the FBI's organized crime division, lamented that "with all this media coverage [Gotti] is beginning to look like a folk hero."[38]

———

Frank Costello visited the barbershop at the *Waldorf Astoria*, a luxurious New York hotel, every day. While he was shaved, manicured, had his hair cut, and his shoes shined, countless political and criminal figures waited in the corridor, hoping for a chance to speak with him. Although the location was far from discreet, Costello knew the constant background noise would foil any police attempts to eavesdrop on his conversations[39].

———

Joseph Bonanno, boss of the Bonanno family, was a cultured man who could recite passages from Dante's *Divine Comedy* or Machiavelli's *The Prince* by heart[40]. His mob associates even complained that he used words they couldn't understand when speaking Italian[41].

Bootlegger Georges Remus placed great importance on his image. He frequented the gym, wore a hat to hide his baldness[42], and always referred to himself in the third person[43]. Eager to win the favor of Cincinnati's high society, he hosted lavish parties at his twenty-room mansion, whose entrance was guarded by two lion statues worth four thousand dollars each. He also owned a collection of rare manuscripts, including one signed by George Washington, an exotic tree garden, marble sculptures, oriental rugs, and even gave his adopted daughter a piano adorned with gold leaf[44]. Guests were typically welcomed with a hundred-dollar bill tucked under their plates and could sip the finest champagne by a Roman-style pool, complete with live musicians and aquatic performers. To top it off, Remus delighted his guests with gifts of jewelry and brand-new Pontiac cars[45].

Benjamin Siegel enjoyed going to bed early, after applying a moisturizing cream and securing an elastic band around his chin to prevent his face from sagging. He also slept with an eye mask[46].

Lucky Luciano learned proper etiquette under the tutelage of Arnold Rothstein, the brilliant crime financier. Thanks to his wise guidance, the young man from the Lower East Side discovered how to use table cutlery, open doors for women, and help them sit by holding their chairs. Luciano often lamented that Rothstein hadn't lived longer to make him even more refined[47].

Sam Giancana collected antiques, with a particular interest in earthenware items and paintings. During his travels, he often stopped by specialty stores and made efforts to understand different forms of artistic expression[48]. In painting, his tastes evolved from realism to the more abstract realms of cubism[49]. The boss of the Outfit was so absorbed by his passion that he didn't hesitate to punish his daughter with a belt whenever she accidentally knocked over one of his precious porcelain figurines[50]. Upon his death, his extensive collection was auctioned off by Chicago art galleries[51].

CRIME

Carlo Gambino in 1930, New York Police Department

Roy DeMeo, a ruthless hitman for the Gambino family, showed more tenderness toward animals than toward his fellow human beings. Despite having executed over two hundred people with his crew[52], the mobster surprisingly enjoyed playing with sparrows and even once helped a frog that had wandered into his garden. Growing fond of the amphibian, he built it a small shelter and would feed it every morning before heading off to fulfill his contracts[53]. Tragically, a gardener he had hired accidentally ran over the frog with a lawnmower. According to his son Albert, DeMeo "was purple with rage," saying he "had never seen him like that" and that "there were tears in his eyes." Mourning the loss, DeMeo gave the frog a proper burial beneath a tree[54].

Benjamin Siegel attempted to sell explosives to Benito Mussolini, then the Italian head of government, in 1938. After attending a private demonstration of a new devastating substance called "Atomite," Countess Di Frasso, Siegel's lover, signed a $50,000 contract granting her the rights to commercialize the product in exchange for a percentage of the profits. Tempted by the promise of a groundbreaking weapon, Mussolini sent the couple an advance of $40,000 and invited them to Rome to present Atomite to military officials[55]. Unfortunately, once there, the demonstration failed spectacularly. Irritated, the "Duce" demanded his money back, threatening Siegel and Di Frasso with imprisonment if they didn't comply. Worse, he ordered them to leave their comfortable villa suite and spend the night in the stables. To add insult to injury, Siegel discovered that Mussolini gifted their former accommodations to two high-ranking members of the Third Reich: Joseph Goebbels, Minister of Propaganda, and Hermann Göring, Hitler's Air Force Chief[56]. A staunch anti-Nazi, Siegel considered assassinating them in their sleep but ultimately decided against it due to the immense risk. He regretted this decision for the rest of his life[57].

While dining at a restaurant in Queens, Paul Vario, a lieutenant of the Lucchese family, held back from reacting when the maître d' accidentally spilled wine on his wife's dress. However, when the clumsy server began getting too close to her curves while wiping her with a dirty rag, the mobster exploded with rage and started beating him violently. The maître d' managed to escape into the kitchen under the protection of his co-workers[58]. Determined not to let it slide, Vario summoned reinforcements and had all the waitstaff and kitchen hands beaten with baseball bats as they left work[59].

Joseph P. Kennedy, father of future U.S. President John F. Kennedy, was partnered with Frank Costello in a bootlegging operation during Prohibition. The two men imported Scotch and Irish whiskey into New York State and New England. However, when Kennedy attempted to expand his business into Detroit, a local gang placed a bounty on his head, angered by his stepping on their toes. Fortunately, two of Capone's enforcers, Paul "The Waiter" Ricca and Murray "The Camel" Humphreys, intervened on his behalf and canceled the contract that threatened his life[60].

A member of the mafia can be killed by their own crime family if they commit any of the following offenses:

- Failing to share the profits from their activities with their superiors[61] (the cut could be as high as eighty percent of the earnings[62]).
- Disrespecting another mafioso, whether by mocking their mother[63], striking them, or sleeping with their wife, mistress, or daughter[64].
- Being homosexual. For example, John "Johnny Boy" D'Amato, a lieutenant in the DeCavalcante family, was executed after his girlfriend spread rumors that he preferred men[65].
- Refusing to obey a superior's order[66].
- Speaking ill of the boss[67].
- Breaking the omerta by discussing mafia activities with anyone outside the organization[68].

Enoch "Nucky" Johnson began his career on the right side of the law as a deputy sheriff under his father. After succeeding him, he eventually rose to the position of treasurer of Atlantic County[69].

However, bolstered by his growing influence and various activities, he began accepting bribes from establishments seeking to open gambling halls or operate brothels[70]. The politician also made sure to take a percentage of every liter of alcohol sold during Prohibition, boasting annual earnings of nearly $500,000[71]. In cahoots with the New York mafia, he allowed bootleggers to receive their shipments at the city's port[72] and graciously hosted the infamous Atlantic City Conference in 1929[73], which laid the groundwork for a national crime syndicate. Ultimately convicted of tax evasion in 1939, he was sentenced to ten years in prison. Upon his release, Johnson found himself alone and penniless, with only $258 to his name[74].

———

Dutch Schultz recommended that his men pour fresh cement into the eyes of his opponents to blind them[75].

———

Charles Gagliodotto and Davie Petillo, hitmen for the Genovese family, dressed as women to avoid drawing attention from their targets. Donning hats, dresses, and concealing pistols in handbags, they managed to kill a dozen people without being caught. Their most audacious hit took place at a funeral, where, hidden behind black veils, they entered the limousine of one of the attendees and executed him at point-blank range[76].

Unlike popular belief, the Mafia is not a single entity controlled by one man. It is rather a constellation of criminal groups adhering to the same codes and traditions, such as the law of omerta[77]. However, it is true that a national commission was established in 1931 to streamline relations between families, coordinate certain rackets, and safeguard shared interests[78].

Meyer Lansky led violent raids against Nazi sympathizers in the United States[79]. Born Meyer Suchowljansky in the Jewish town of Grodno, then under Russian rule[80], he faced rampant antisemitism from an early age, marked by pogroms and discrimination[81]. Shaped by this harrowing past, Lansky took pride in fighting supporters of the Third Reich with a team of Jewish gangsters, rejecting any assistance from his Italian friends. He later remarked that he had "enjoyed beating up those Nazis," that he treated "big antisemites in a very special way," and that he taught them that "Jews couldn't be kicked around."[82]

Sam Giancana, boss of Chicago's Outfit, was a member of a group of forty-two young criminals in his youth: the "42 Gang." The name was, in fact, a nod to the book *Ali Baba and the Forty Thieves*. Over the years, the gang grew to nearly five hundred members and supplied many soldiers to the mafia[83].

Vito Genovese donated $250,000 dollars to the fascist party of Nola, Italy. In return, he was granted the title of "Commendatore," the highest civilian honor under Mussolini's regime[84]. However, when World War II began to favor the Allied forces, Genovese quickly renounced his honorary title and distanced himself from his far-right connections. Hoping to end the war on the winning side, he offered his services as a guide and translator to American troops stationed in the Naples area[85]. With access to the military base, he began stealing trucks and filling them with supplies from the warehouses to profit from the black market. Unaware of his schemes, Captain Charles Dunn wrote him a glowing letter of recommendation in 1944, describing Genovese as an "invaluable" asset and "absolutely honest."[86] Riding on this image of a patriotic helper, the mobster hypocritically denounced other criminals engaging in black market activities to take over their operations. Despite the mounting suspicions against him, Genovese was never convicted and smoothly resumed his mafia dealings in New York after the war[87].

Suspected of giving information to law enforcement[88], Bruno Facciola, a soldier of the Lucchese family, was stabbed and then executed with six bullets to the head and chest. Once dead, the corpse of a canary was placed in his mouth. The message intended for the other mafiosi was clear: absolute prohibition on talking to the police[89].

The Los Angeles mafia was held in low regard by law enforcement. Daryl Gates, the chief of police in the City of Angels, even nicknamed the organization the "Mickey Mouse Mafia" and launched Operation "Lightweight" to imprison twenty of its members in 1984[90].

Before taking control of the richest and most powerful mafia family in the United States, Carlo Gambino did not command much respect among his peers in organized crime. For example, Joseph Bonanno described him as "a squirrel of a man, a servile and cringing individual." Bonanno even claimed to have seen Albert Anastasia almost slap Gambino without eliciting any reaction[91]. However, Gambino redeemed himself spectacularly, leading a thousand men and countless rackets with success for over fifty years[92].

Jimmy Burke, an associate of the Lucchese family, ordered the execution of his best friend Remo after he tipped off the police about one of Burke's smuggled cigarette shipments[93]. Despite Remo having recently gifted him a trip to Florida for his wedding anniversary[94], Burke could never forgive the betrayal. He had him strangled in his car and buried under a concrete slab near a bocce court in Queens. Every time Burke visited the court to play, he would sarcastically call out to his old friend, "Hi Remo, how ya doing?"[95]

The vast majority of executions ordered by the mafia target its own members or people in business with it[96]. A contract is issued by the boss or captains and cannot, under any circumstances, be refused by the one tasked with carrying it out, even if the victim is a close family member[97]. Murders most often take place in a car or the back room of a restaurant. The favorite method among New York mobsters is to put two bullets behind the condemned person's ear[98].

DOLLARS

Al Capone interviewed at the Chicago Detective Bureau

Paul Vario loved paying for outings with his wife using a stolen credit card. Despite his considerable financial means, the mobster embraced the risk of getting caught to experience the thrilling sensation of swindling someone and getting away with it. Neither the music, the meal, nor even his wife could provide him with as much satisfaction as the act of theft[99].

To reward Joseph Pistone for successfully infiltrating the Bonanno family from 1976 to 1981, the FBI granted him a bonus of $500. A laughable amount considering the enormous dangers faced by the agent, who risked his life every day posing as Donnie Brasco, a supposed jewel thief. Thanks to the valuable information Pistone gathered, the government was able to indict two hundred gangsters and send half of them to prison[100]. Infuriated by this betrayal, mafia bosses placed a $500,000 bounty on his head[101].

In 1938, Benjamin Siegel embarked on an incredible treasure hunt in Costa Rica. A few months earlier, the gangster had studied a map roughly sketched on a napkin by a man named Bill Bowbeer. It marked the location of a fabulous treasure, estimated at $90 million, buried in the sands of Cocos Island[102]. Allured by the scent of money, Siegel boarded a three-masted schooner, the *Metha Nelson*, accompanied by his lover, Countess Dorothy Di Frasso, and twenty crew members[103]. Unfortunately, the search was unsuccessful. After ten grueling days battling torrential rain, sweltering heat, and swarms of insects, Siegel and his companions had to throw in the towel[104].

Gregory Scarpa Sr., a lieutenant in the Colombo family and an informant for the FBI, always made sure to carry $5,000 in cash in case he needed to bribe someone[105].

John Gotti lived in a modest home in Howard Beach, Queens, and claimed to earn only $25,000 a year as a salesman for a plumbing supply company[106]. A laughable tax declaration, considering he made between $5 and $13 million annually[107].

———

Perhaps following an eerie premonition, Arnold Rothstein took out a $50,000 life insurance policy (approximately $900,000 in 2025)[108] just two days before his death on November 6, 1928[109].

———

In 1949, Frank Costello was appointed vice president of the Salvation Army's men's division. He began his role by organizing a $100-a-plate charity dinner at the *Copacabana*, an upscale New York nightclub[110]. The menu featured chicken soup, filet of beef with green beans, and a fresh fruit cocktail. However, the media was uncomfortable with a gangster leading such a respectable institution and harshly criticized the questionable sources of some donations[111]. Under pressure, Costello resigned just one month after taking the position[112].

———

Meyer Lansky only swore by cash, which was harder to trace than bank transfers. He owned five safe-deposit boxes in New York, Newark, Boston, and Hollywood. All his deposits were exclusively made with bills or coins[113].

———

In 1992, the waste collection company Browning-Ferris Industries attempted to establish itself in New York without submitting to the Mafia, which tightly controlled the industry. In response to this affront, their sales manager found the decapitated head of a dog in his yard. A note was tucked in the mouth of the poor animal: "Welcome to New York."[114]

———

On November 10, 1986, the renowned *Fortune* magazine dedicated its cover and a full feature to the fifty most powerful mobsters of the time. In response to the question, "How they rank in wealth, power, and influence?" the magazine offered the following top three:

1- Anthony "Fat Tony" Salerno, front boss of the Genovese family.

2- Anthony "Big Tuna" Accardo, boss of Chicago's Outfit.

3- Anthony "Tony Ducks" Corallo, boss of the Lucchese family[115].

Sadly, Salerno didn't get to enjoy his top spot for long. Two months later, he was sentenced to a hundred years in prison for his role in a criminal organisation[116].

The opulent lifestyle of Paul Castellano starkly contrasted with Carlo Gambino's, his predecessor as head of the Gambino family. While Don Carlo was content with a modest Brooklyn home, Castellano built a lavish $3.5 million mansion atop Staten Island's highest hill. Nicknamed the "White House" by mobsters, the property offered stunning views of New York's Upper Bay. However, the house was so massive that water pressure dropped significantly on the upper floors[117]. Fortunately, the interior decor made up for this minor inconvenience with Carrara marble, exquisite silk, and rococo furnishings. To top it off, the garden even featured an Olympic-sized swimming pool[118].

Al Capone earned approximately $100 million a year through the six thousands speakeasies he controlled in the Chicago area. To ensure the money kept flowing despite Prohibition, "Scarface" didn't hesitate to bribe the police, paying nearly $500,000 a month to keep officers compliant[119]. One city councilman even later admitted that Chicago was "the only completely corrupt city in America."[120]

In the 1960s, a report from the U.S. Department of Justice estimated that the mafia generated annual revenues of between $7 billion and $10 billion (around $105 billion in 2025). This staggering amount equaled the combined revenues of America's ten largest companies at the time: General Motors, Standard Oil, U.S. Steel, Ford, General

Electric, IBM, Mobil Oil, Texaco, and Chrysler. In a wiretapped conversation, Meyer Lansky once confided to his wife his satisfaction with a cryptic sentence: "We're bigger than U.S. Steel."[121]

Nicknamed "The Big Bankroll," Arnold Rothstein lent money at exorbitant interest rates, sometimes as high as forty-eight percent[122]. His debtors included speakeasies[123] and even the Russian Communist Party[124]. Occasionally, he played the benefactor, waiving interest in exchange for a share of the profits, as he did when financing transatlantic liquor smuggling operations[125]. At the height of his wealth, Rothstein's fortune was estimated at over $1.7 million. By the time of his death, however, he had only about $56,000 left—and more than $490,000 in debts[126].

While Frank Costello was under close medical observation at Roosevelt Hospital after narrowly escaping an assassination attempt[127], a police officer took advantage of his temporary weakness to steal

$3,200 from his jacket. Costello never filed a complaint[128].

If New York City real estate is now infamous for its exorbitant prices, the mafia played a part in this reputation. Between 1970 and the early 1980s[129], all construction companies securing contracts over $2 million indeed had to pay a percentage to the Five Families to work without trouble[130]. Concrete prices were also inflated by up to seventy percent by mob-linked suppliers, driving project costs sky-high. Several iconic buildings, including the *Trump Tower*, the *IBM Building*, and the *Helmsley Palace Hotel* (now the *Lotte New York Palace Hotel*), fell victim to this lucrative racket[131].

JUSTICE

Frank Costello testifying before the Kefauver Committee

Frank Costello had enormous political influence, to the point of being able to get judges elected. Between 1940 and 1945, most of New York's magistrates needed the powerful mobster's approval before taking office. One of the most notable cases involved Thomas Aurelio, then candidate for the New York Supreme Court. In 1943, wiretaps revealed that Costello had persuaded Democratic Party officials to give their full backing to Aurelio's campaign[132]. After his election, Aurelio assured his benefactor of his "undying loyalty."[133]

In August 1964, Gregory Scarpa Sr. helped the U.S. government locate the bodies of three civil rights activists murdered by the Ku Klux Klan. Their disappearance had become a national scandal, and the FBI's inability to recover the victims prompted agents to turn to the mobster, who had recently been enlisted as a secret informant[134]. Scarpa kidnapped a KKK member, who happened to be the mayor of a small town, and used brutal methods to extract information. First, he shoved a loaded pistol into the man's mouth, threatening to blow his head off. Then, he unzipped the mayor's pants, held a razor close, and warned that he'd castrate him. Terrified, the mayor quickly revealed the burial site of the three activists[135].

James Capone, Al Capone's older brother, was a lawman. After serving in the U.S. Army during World War I, he participated in several operations against alcohol smugglers upon his return home. To avoid complications, he changed his name to Richard James Hart, in honor of his favorite movie star, William Hart. In 1926, he shifted his career path, becoming a special agent for the Bureau of Indian Affairs in South Dakota. A staunch defender of the law, he was credited with the arrest of at least twenty murderers[136].

For ten years, George Cassiday sold bootleg alcohol to members of Congress—the very people who had voted for Prohibition. Known as "the man in the green hat," he was finally arrested for his activities in 1930. Hoping to capitalize on his unusual experience, he wrote a series of explosive articles for *The Washington Post*, revealing that four out of five senators regularly consumed alcohol[137].

The CIA tried to enlist the mafia to assassinate Cuban President Fidel Castro. The revolutionary had just overthrown Fulgencio Batista, a U.S.-friendly leader. Declassified agency archives from 2007 reveal that high-level emissaries met with Chicago gangster John "Handsome Johnny" Roselli in a New York hotel on September 14, 1960, to discuss the matter. The CIA indeed knew that the casinos and hotels owned by the mafia in Havana were declining due to the exodus of tourists and that the interests of both camps converged. The agency offered $150,000 for the head of the "Líder Máximo." Sam Giancana, boss of the Chicago Outfit, joined the effort, suggesting poison as a quieter alternative to bullets. But the assassin he selected, a Cuban official named Juan Orta, abandoned the mission after several failed attempts[138]. The operation ended in 1961 with the Bay of Pigs invasion[139].

After proving his worth by generating significant profits for a family or committing a murder on its behalf[140], an Italian man may aspire to join its ranks[141]. This lengthy process, validated by a recommendation from an established mobster and the boss's approval[142], culminates in a highly ritualized ceremony. Surrounded by his future colleagues, the candidate must first pretend ignorance of why he's been summoned to the secret meeting. Then, after agreeing to kill on command, his index finger is pricked, allowing his blood to drip onto a piece of paper[143] or the image of a saint[144]. The bloodstained object is set ablaze while the candidate recites the ancient oath of Cosa Nostra: "You live by the gun and the knife, and you die by the gun and the knife. And if I betray anyone in this room, or any friend of ours, may my soul burn in hell like this paper." Once these grim words are spoken, the future soldier is kissed on both cheeks by the ceremony leader and officially introduced as a full-fledged member to those present. The participants then form a circle, holding hands, as the boss reiterates the organization's fundamental rules—the most important being that "this family comes before your family."[145]

Israel refused to allow Meyer Lansky to settle on its soil despite the *Law of Return*. This 1950 legislation permits any Jewish person to immigrate and receive a certificate to live and work in the country[146]. Lansky, seeking refuge from a U.S. trial for tax fraud[147], saw it as a golden opportunity. But despite his anti-Nazi efforts and fundraising for Israel[148], his visa application was denied under Section 2(b)(3) of the *Law of Return*[149], which excludes individuals with a criminal past[150].

The mobster hearings conducted by the U.S. Senate's Special Committee to Investigate Crime in Interstate Commerce, more commonly known as the "Kefauver Committee," captivated over thirty million Americans in March 1951[151]. The record-breaking audience surpassed that of a season of the hit sitcom *The Big Bang Theory*[152]. Over six hundred witnesses, including Frank Costello himself, were called to testify in fourteen cities across the country[153].

John Gotti earned the nickname "Teflon Don" for his ability to win trial after trial[154]. But behind these acquittals lay a darker reality. Romual Piecyk, a refrigeration mechanic beaten and robbed by Gotti after asking him to move his car[155], faced relentless intimidation to silence him. Anonymous calls, brake tampering, and menacing tails sent a clear message: Piecyk fled the city[156], eventually clearing Gotti's name[157] after being forcibly brought to court by the police[158]. George Pape, a juror in Gotti's 1987 trial[159], was also bribed with $60,000 to ensure the Gambino family boss avoided prison[160].

Georges Remus, a criminal defense attorney[161] and pharmacist from Chicago[162], became one of the most prominent bootleggers in the United States by exploiting a legal loophole. After carefully studying the *Volstead Act*, the law enforcing Prohibition from 1920 to 1933, he discovered that the production and sale of medicinal whiskey were curiously allowed under government licensing[163]. He thus quickly bought his first distillery and began illegally diverting the valuable liquor to the black market[164]. Remus supplied several major crime figures, including Johnny Torrio, Al Capone, and Arnold Rothstein, and prided himself on not diluting his products with water[165]. His earnings were estimated at nearly $20 million[166]. This legal flexibility also benefited Winston Churchill, who held a medical certificate permitting him to drink alcohol in the U.S. during Prohibition. While visiting New York to deliver a series of lectures in December 1931, the future British Prime Minister was hit by a car on Fifth Avenue. He sustained a fractured nose, broken ribs, and a lung infection. After a brief recovery in the Bahamas, Churchill returned to New York with his precious certificate, in which Dr. Pickhardt explicitly recommended that he drink at least 8.4 ounces of alcohol per day[167].

Frank Gusenberg, a member of Bugs Moran's gang, upheld the code of omerta to his dying breath. On February 14, 1929, Gusenberg and four other gangsters were in a North Clark Street warehouse inspecting a whiskey shipment, unaware they were living their final moments[168]. A hit squad sent by Al Capone, disguised as police officers, confronted them and ruthlessly gunned them down with Thompson M1921. When the real police arrived to survey the carnage, only two members of Moran's gang were still alive. One of them was Frank Gusenberg. Fiercely opposed to collaborating with the enemy, he denied anyone had shot him. The next day, the press seized on the story, dubbing it the "Saint Valentine's Day Massacre."[169]

Anthony "Big Tuna" Accardo, boss of the Chicago Outfit[170], invoked the Fifth Amendment of the U.S. Constitution one hundred seventy-two consecutive times during the Senate's anti-racketeering committee hearings in 1958. The Fifth Amendment allows an accused person to remain silent if they believe a question might incriminate them[171].

When asked whether he had any respect for the government, Accardo remained perfectly silent[172].

J. Edgar Hoover, the legendary founder and director of the FBI from 1935 to 1972, curiously hindered efforts to combat the mafia until the 1950s. He refused to protect witnesses, avoided opening investigations on the topic, and even tried to block the Senate's 1951 special committee on organized crime[173]. This paradoxical behavior from such a staunch lawman could be explained by several blackmail attempts orchestrated by mobsters. First, Hoover, an avid horse racing gambler[174], regularly received insider tips about rigged races from the mafia through a trusted intermediary. Frank Costello later told his lawyer that Hoover "will never know how many races [he] had to fix for those lousy ten-dollar bets."[175] Meyer Lansky, meanwhile, reportedly ensured Hoover's compliance using compromising photographs of the very puritanical[176] FBI director engaged in a homosexual act with his lover, Clyde Tolson[177]. Lansky also often bragged in private that "Hoover had been fixed."[178]

The *Racketeer Influenced and Corrupt Organization Act* (RICO) is widely suspected of being named to honor the mobster character Rico from the film *Little Caesar*. Released in 1931, this cult movie tells the story of a gangster clawing his way to the top of organized crime in Chicago. G. Robert Blakey, one of the key architects of the law, always refused to confirm or deny whether this cinematic homage was intentional[179]. Thanks to this new legal provision signed by Richard Nixon in 1970[180], law enforcement finally gained the ability to prosecute mafia bosses by demonstrating their involvement in crimes committed by their subordinates[181].

Al Capone was convicted not for any of the two hundred murders in which he was suspected of involvement[182], nor for extortion or his illicit businesses, but for… tax fraud. A few years earlier, the U.S. Supreme Court had ruled that illicit income was subject to taxation[183], leaving Capone unable to settle his taxes without admitting his illegal activities. The indictment report against him spanned three thousand six hundred and eighty pages. After eight hours and ten minutes of deliberation, the jury found him guilty[184], sentencing him to eleven long years in prison[185].

After winning his trial in 1987, John Gotti was spotted cruising off the Florida coast aboard a cigarette boat bearing the bold inscription "Not Guilty."[186]

In his days as a criminal lawyer, George Remus wasn't afraid to use astonishing strategies in court. During the trial of a man accused of poisoning his wife, for instance, he drank the entire bottle of the supposed lethal liquid in front of the jury. The demonstration was meant to prove that the alleged murder weapon was harmless and that the husband was therefore innocent. Convinced they were about to witness Remus collapse after such bravado, the courtroom was stunned when he continued his plea without showing the slightest sign of distress. What they didn't know was that Remus, thanks to his background in pharmacology, had injected himself with an antidote before performing his daring act. Fifteen minutes later, the defendant walked out of the courtroom, cleared of all charges[187].

FBI agent Joseph Pistone's infiltration of the mafia was so successful that law enforcement officers, unaware of his mission, mistook him for a genuine gangster. Operating under the alias Donnie Brasco, Pistone found himself trailed by car, stopped[188], and even photographed by his own colleagues. On occasion, some officers also presented his photos to other mobsters in an attempt to gather intelligence about him[189].

ODDITIES

Joe Profaci in 1959

Meyer Lansky possessed remarkable intelligence, to the point that an FBI agent once admitted with admiration that "he would have been chairman of the board of General Motors if he'd gone into legitimate business."[190] A mental math enthusiast, the gangster was also a member of the library's book-of-the-month club[191]. He particularly enjoyed history books and biographies, eventually even taking up philosophy in his later years. However, his taste for scholarly texts didn't always resonate with those around him. After Lansky gave him a book on economics, attorney Joseph Varon admitted he "had to stop on the second page" and "couldn't understand a word of it."[192] Lansky also had an extraordinary memory, capable of reciting Shakespeare's *The Merchant of Venice* by heart[193].

Although he led one of New York's Five Families for nearly three decades, Joe Profaci was paradoxically a devout Catholic. His sprawling thirty-room mansion, once owned by Theodore Roosevelt, even housed a chapel. The altar inside was an exact replica of the one in St. Peter's Basilica in Rome. Profaci was also a proud member of the

Knights of Columbus, a Christian charitable organization. Unfortunately, his apparent piety often gave way to his darker nature. On one occasion, Profaci flew into a rage upon learning that a drug addict had stolen jewelry from a statue of the Virgin Mary in his parish church. Determined to punish the blasphemer, he had the man kidnapped and tortured to death for hours[194].

Frank Costello regularly visited the Central Park Zoo to watch the monkeys. One day, perhaps annoyed by being stared at so intently, one of them spat in his face. Surprisingly, the powerful gangster grew fond of the little primate, often inquiring about its health whenever he noticed its absence from the cages[195].

Although he was one of the greatest bootleggers during Prohibition, Arnold Rothstein didn't drink. His beverage of choice was milk, which he consumed in abundance[196]. Rothstein was also highly concerned about his health, particularly his digestion. Alongside his sobriety, he didn't smoke and ate industrial quantities of figs[197].

Carmine Galante, the unofficial boss of the Bonanno family, was rarely seen without a cigar in his mouth. Unsurprisingly, his nicknames included "The Cigar" and "Lilo" (a Sicilian term for cigar)[198].

Rocco Fischetti, cousin of Al Capone and a Chicago mobster[199], enjoyed playing with model trains in his home. He had designed and built a superb set, where miniature locomotives traversed pastoral landscapes of villages, mountains, and coal mines. His masterpiece had cost him several thousand dollars, and his perfectionism led him to include animated figurines of rail workers[200]. Fischetti delighted in donning an engineer's cap and showing off his creation to his mafia friends and their children[201].

Benjamin "Lefty" Ruggiero, a Bonanno family mobster, owned a pet lion cub. Though he never gave it a name, Ruggiero was very fond of the animal and even took it for car rides. However, when the cub's claws began tearing through his leather seats, the gangster had to arrange for it to be kept at a mafia-run club[202]. Eventually, the lion grew so large that it was moved to a warehouse. Unfortunately, due to the damage it caused and food costs reaching two hundred dollars a day, Ruggiero decided to abandon it by chaining it to a park bench. The next morning, the ASPCA (an American animal welfare organization) rescued the lion, and the *New York Post* informed its readers that "the king of the jungle had been found in Queens."[203]

Al Capone traveled in an armored Cadillac Sedan[204]. After his conviction in 1931[205], the vehicle was seized by the IRS (the American tax authority) and repurposed to transport President Franklin D. Roosevelt between 1941 and 1942[206].

Many of the most prominent mafia bosses in history are buried just a few feet apart at St. John Cemetery in New York. This 19th-century Catholic site is indeed the final resting place of Carlo Gambino, Joe Profaci, Carmine Galante, Joe Colombo, Lucky Luciano, and Vito Genovese[207].

Alphonse "Little Al" D'Arco, interim boss of the Lucchese family and the first mafia leader to testify for the U.S. government, began his career as a U.S. Air Force soldier in Alaska. His job was to monitor an airstrip for twelve months[208]. Following an excellent service record, he was invited to take the officer school entrance exam. His score was so high that he was accused of cheating and had to retake the test, earning an even better score. Unfortunately, he ultimately declined the opportunity and returned to New York, where his career took a far less honorable turn[209].

John Gotti had a fear of flying. After winning his 1987 trial, he chose to travel to Fort Lauderdale,

Florida[210], for a vacation by taking the train down the entire East Coast rather than spending a few hours in the air[211]. Years later, however, he was forced to board a chartered flight to serve a life sentence at the Marion federal penitentiary in Illinois[212].

Benjamin Siegel hated his nickname "Bugsy." Only actor George Raft was allowed to call him that, though Raft preferred to avoid conflict and affectionately nicknamed him "Baby Blue Eyes," a sobriquet much better suited to the gangster[213]. Even journalists were careful with their words. When Siegel purchased advertising space to promote his *Flamingo* casino in *Las Vegas Life* magazine, a note was posted in the newsroom: "From this day forward, Mr. Siegel of the Flamingo will never be referred to as 'Bugsy'. Make it Ben or Benjamin."[214]

Frank Costello meticulously tended to his fruit trees and rose bushes. Proud of his gardening skills, he sometimes displayed his roses at horticultural fairs, winning several awards that brought him great satisfaction[215].

———

Frankie Yale, one of Al Capone's earliest crime employers[216], received a first-class burial at New York's Holy Cross Cemetery. The funeral procession included ten thousand mourners, thirty-eight flower-filled cars, and two hundred fifty vehicles escorting the gangster's body to its final resting place[217]. Around the grave, one hundred twelve men holding a single rose each watched as gravediggers covered Yale's $15,000 silver casket with earth[218].

———

Al Capone attended the same school as Lucky Luciano: *Public School 7* in Brooklyn. Both men were taught by the same teacher, Sadie Mulvaney[219]. While Capone managed a respectable B average through sixth grade, he eventually had to repeat a year due to struggles in grammar and arithmetic. After being reprimanded by a teacher for increasing absenteeism, Capone punched the instructor and was immediately expelled at the age of just fourteen[220].

The Roman Catholic Archdiocese of New York refused to hold a funeral mass for Carmine Galante, fearing the scandal such an event would provoke. Albert Anastasia faced a similar refusal upon his death in 1957 and was buried in unconsecrated ground. However, other notorious mobsters, such as Dutch Schultz and Joe Gallo, were granted proper Catholic funerals[221].

Dominick "Sonny Black" Napolitano, a lieutenant in the Bonanno family, had a deep passion for pigeons. He owned ninety-five bird and affectionately spoke to them during visits to the rooftop of his apartment. Each one was well-fed with quality food and given a name[222]. Tragically, when the bosses of New York's Five Families discovered that he had unwittingly allowed FBI agent Joseph D. Pistone, alias Donnie Brasco, into their ranks, Napolitano was brutally executed. His hands were severed, and his body, found three months later in the Staten Island marshes, was so decomposed that the morgue needed weeks to confirm his identity. Sensing his imminent demise, Napolitano had handed the keys to his apartment to the bartender of the *Motion Lounge*, a mob-owned club beneath his residence, to ensure his cherished birds would be cared for. A week after his disappearance, the pigeon coop was dismantled—a clear sign to Pistone that Napolitano was dead[223].

―

Despite the many crimes he committed while leading the Bonanno family, Joseph Bonanno declared in his later years that his greatest regret was never mastering the English language[224].

―

Before becoming one of the most infamous crime bosses in American history, Al Capone worked a series of surprising odd jobs, including as a clerk in a candy store, installing pinball machines in a bowling alley, and cutting paper and clothes in a bindery[225].

———

Dean O'Bannion, head of the gang rivaling Johnny Torrio and Al Capone, ran his operations out of his Chicago flower shop, *Schofield's Flowers*. Despite his criminal activities—robberies, thefts, bootlegging, and murders—O'Bannion had a passion for bouquets and the church, where he even served as an altar boy. His talent as a florist made him the go-to supplier for mobster funerals[226]. He was assassinated in his shop on the morning of November 10, 1924, while trimming chrysanthemums[227].

———

Arnold Rothstein harbored a deep hatred for his older brother, Harry. When Arnold was three years old, his father caught him coldly staring at Harry as he slept, a knife in hand. No one knows what might have happened without this providential intervention. In a twist of fate, Rothstein was buried right next to his despised brother in New York's Union Field Cemetery[228].

———

Despite being one of the most powerful mob bosses, Frank Costello refused to hire a driver for his many meetings, choosing instead to walk or take a taxi like any ordinary New Yorker. Fearless, he also never employed a bodyguard[229].

———

The University of Chicago owns the *Argos Lectionary*, a compilation of one hundred and forty-five extremely rare biblical parchments dating back to the 9th or 10th century[230]. This historical treasure was purchased in 1930 from the owner of Big Jim Colosimo's former restaurant. According to the seller, the book was once used to swear in new members of the Chicago Outfit[231].

———

The ace of spades is considered an unlucky card by mafiosi. This superstition traces back to the murder of Joe "The Boss" Masseria by Lucky Luciano on April 15, 1931[232]. After playing cards with his boss at a Coney Island restaurant, Luciano excused himself to the restroom[233], leaving four gunmen to execute Masseria with multiple bullets to the head, back, and chest[234]. When found on the floor, Masseria was clutching an ace of spades in his right hand[235].

Frank Costello had a particular fondness for Broadway critic Mark Hellinger because, unlike his colleagues who attended shows for free, Hellinger insisted on paying for his own tickets. However, Costello's admiration sometimes went overboard. Upon learning that Hellinger had broken his leg after falling from a boat, Costello sent so many flowers to his hospital room that the journalist eventually complained[236].

The infamous *Ravenite Club*, a gathering spot for mafiosi to discuss criminal activities[237], eventually became a clothing store in the 2000s. Perhaps as a nod to the gangsters who once occupied the building at 247 Mulberry Street in New York, the store is named *Descendant of Thieves*[238]. After all, the club was frequented by Lucky Luciano[239] and later served as the Gambino family headquarters under

John Gotti[240]. After Gotti's arrest in 1991, the government seized the *Ravenite* a few years later and auctioned it for just over a million dollars to an investment fund[241].

HEALTH

Tommy Lucchese in 1958, Associated Press

To avoid prison, Vincent "The Chin" Gigante feigned insanity. He wandered Greenwich Village in pajamas, urinated in the street, and muttered incomprehensible gibberish to himself. The boss of the Genovese family was so convincing in his act that he even collected $900 a month in government disability benefits for his supposed mental condition[242]. His ruse worked from 1990 to 1997, when testimony from a mafia turncoat proved his mental health was intact[243]. Gigante was sentenced to twelve years in prison and fined $1.25 million[244].

Peter "Fat Pete" Chiodo, a lieutenant in the Lucchese family, miraculously survived an assassination attempt thanks to his size. Suspected of being a snitch by his boss, Anthony "Gaspipe" Casso[245], Chiodo was ambushed at a Staten Island gas station by a hit team[246]. The twelve bullets that tore through his flesh failed to hit any vital organs, which were well protected[247] by his four hundred pound frame[248]. After a long stay in intensive care[249], Chiodo retaliated by cooperating with the government, becoming the first Lucchese family member to publicly break omerta[250].

Frank Costello had polyps removed from his vocal cords in his youth. Unfortunately, the surgery went poorly, leaving his voice permanently altered with a distinctive gravelly tone. "One doctor wanted to cut them off, another advised burning them off. I went with the wrong doctor" he philosophized[251]. However, his new voice became a boon for actor Marlon Brando, who drew heavy inspiration from it to play the iconic role of Vito Corleone in *The Godfather*. Indeed, Brando studied recordings of Costello's testimony before the Kefauver Commission, which was investigating organized crime in the United States, perfecting his craft and immortalizing the mobster's raspy voice[252].

Anna Citron, Meyer Lansky's wife, suffered from dementia. Doctors linked her symptoms to schizophrenia, and she endured numerous electroshock therapy sessions to alleviate them[253]. Sadly, the treatment failed to improve her condition. Frustrated by mounting medical bills and lacking affection for his wife[254], Lansky filed for divorce on February 14, 1947—Valentine's Day. Left to subsist on a small alimony, Anna gradually deteriorated to the point where she no longer recognized her own children. She ended up wandering the streets of the Upper West Side, among drug addicts and the destitute[255].

By the age of thirty-three, Al Capone suffered from syphilis, gonorrhea[256], and a perforated nasal septum due to heavy cocaine use[257]. While serving time in Alcatraz, his mental health steadily deteriorated, culminating in a feces battle with a neighboring inmate[258]. In his final years, cloistered in his Miami mansion, Capone's cognitive abilities regressed to those of a six-year-old child[259].

Mickey Cohen, a Los Angeles mobster, had an intense fear of germs. He compulsively washed his hands and avoided touching any surface unless it was covered with a cloth. After taking showers multiple times a day, he would carefully lay clean towels on the floor to avoid stepping directly on it. His housekeeper would then sanitize the entire bathroom with alcohol. Cohen also changed his clothes frequently throughout the day, sometimes spending up to three hours preparing himself[260].

———

Tommy Lucchese, boss of the Lucchese family, lost the index finger of his right hand in a mechanical shop accident. Years later, after being arrested for car theft, he was nicknamed "Three-Finger Brown" by the officer taking his fingerprints. The latter was indeed a fan of the baseball player Mordecai Brown[261], who had a successful career with the Chicago Cubs despite having two fingers amputated[262]. The nickname remained, much to Lucchese's displeasure, who couldn't stand being called that[263].

———

Despite the power and wealth it brought, being the boss of a crime family often came with significant health risks. Several mob leaders suffered from severe health issues, including Stefano Magaddino, the Buffalo crime lord, who endured a heart attack, and Tommy Lucchese, who died of a cerebral hemorrhage[264]. Carlo Gambino, experienced a heart attack shortly before his 1967 trial[265], while Joseph Bonanno survived a third heart attack in 1968[266]. Bonanno later described the immense pressures of leadership: "Often in my life, I've had people tell me they wish they were Joe Bonanno, that they had Joe Bonanno's power, his influence, his wealth. Such people don't know what they're talking about. If they want to be like me, they also have to assume the pressures, the anxiety, the tension inherent in my life-style. None of the people who say they want to be Joe Bonanno has ever told me he'd like to have Joe Bonanno's blood pressure."[267]

Gregory Scarpa Sr. died of AIDS due to a contaminated blood transfusion. Suffering from a stomach ulcer worsened by heavy aspirin use to alleviate back pain[268], Scarpa's health sharply deteriorated in August 1986. Admitted to Victory Memorial Hospital, he refused blood from unknown donors, opting instead for that of his Mafia friends[269]. But their hemoglobin was not tested. Paul Mele, a steroid-using bodybuilding associate, unwittingly passed on the fatal infection[270]. Scarpa sued the hospital and won $300,000 in damages in 1992[271].

Sam Giancana sought electroshock therapy[272] to treat his daughter's depression, which had led her to abuse alcohol and sleeping pills[273]. After six months in the hospital, he took her to Hawaii, Mexico, and the Caribbean to help her recover[274].

In 1931, a psychiatric report from Sing-Sing prison assessed Carmine Galante's IQ at ninety. The evaluation also described the future Bonanno family boss as having the mental age of a fourteen-year-old, being timid, ignorant of current events, and possessing a psychopathic personality[275]. Despite this unflattering portrait, Galante went on to speak four languages fluently[276] and successfully lead one of the most powerful criminal organizations in the United States. The whole question is to know who was taking whom for a fool.

———

Frank Costello consulted a psychoanalyst between 1947 and 1949 to deal with an incipient depression. The gangster suffered from his inability to leave the Mafia and fully embrace the refined world of politics, where he felt both comfortable and accomplished[277].

———

Joey Massino, boss of the Bonanno family, possessed a remarkable memory. He could describe with uncanny precision all the FBI agents assigned to surveil him and even recite their license plate numbers from memory[278].

———

Bernard "Buddy" Lansky, Meyer Lansky's eldest son, was born with cerebral palsy. Initially embarrassed by the situation, the gangster distanced himself from his family, only to return determined to provide Buddy with the best care possible. Lansky delved into every book on the subject at the library[279], consulted specialists across the country, and even brought an Austrian surgeon to New York[280]. Through arduous treatments, which required Buddy to be strapped to a board for hours while wearing braces[281], he achieved a relatively normal life. Tragically, after his father's death, Buddy spent his final days in a squalid asylum for the indigent[282], forgotten by everyone, including his own siblings[283].

BEHIND BARS

John Gotti photographed by the FBI in 1990

When the Dannemora prison administration assigned Luciano to the laundry, admiring inmates spontaneously volunteered to take his place. These devoted followers also cleaned his cell and handled all his chores. Luciano even had a valet, Little Davie Betillo, who prepared his favorite meals in a private kitchen provided by the prison administration[284]. In his spare time, Luciano enjoyed playing cards and watching baseball games[285]. However, after being transferred to Great Meadow Prison in 1942[286], the gravity of World War II changed the atmosphere. Eager to track the events, Luciano hung a large map of Europe on his cell wall, carefully marking the Allies' progress and expressing his admiration for General Patton[287].

Al Capone's mother was banned from visiting him at Alcatraz after her corset triggered the metal detector. The decision by the prison administration infuriated the Outfit boss, who tore his work uniform into shreds to vent his anger[288].

James "Whitey" Bulger, the Boston Mafia boss, unknowingly became a subject of the CIA's MKUltra project during his time at the Atlanta penitentiary[289]. MKUltra was a secret program aimed at controlling human behavior through chemical and biological methods[290]. Enticed by the promise of a reduced sentence in exchange for participating in a supposed treatment for schizophrenia, Bulger endured repeated LSD injections over eighteen months. The mental health consequences were dire: he suffered frequent hallucinations and severe insomnia[291]. Of the seventeen other inmates who joined the medical study, many ended up insane or committed suicide[292].

———

John Gotti endured Spartan living conditions at the federal prison in Marion, Illinois. Confined to a four-square-meter cell for twenty-three hours a day, his only possessions were a radio, a small black-and-white television, a cot, a sink, and a toilet. To avoid lying down all day, he twisted his mattress into an "L" shape to fashion a makeshift chair. Last but not least, he was allowed only five visits per month[293].

Joseph Bonanno was treated with the utmost respect during his ninety days detention at Montreal's Bordeaux Prison for lying to immigration authorities[294]. He was served his favorite cognac, Cordon Bleu, fine cigars, and given access to the warden's private phone line. He enjoyed complete freedom of movement and could demand meals of his choice[295]. Far from resenting his preferential treatment, the other inmates were captivated by his reputation as the boss of one of New York's Five Families. They shouted his name, applauded as he passed, and eagerly offered him their services[296].

Santo Trafficante Jr., Florida's organized crime boss, was thrown into Cuban prisons after Fidel Castro's rise to power in 1959[297]. A close ally of former dictator Fulgencio Batista, Trafficante controlled several casinos on the island[298], earning the ire of the "Líder Máximo." While incarcerated, he was visited by Jack Ruby, who would later kill Lee Harvey Oswald, the assassin of President John

F. Kennedy. Upon learning that his execution was imminent, Trafficante scrambled to save his life through any legal or clandestine means available[299]. After weeks of anxiety, he secured his release under mysterious circumstances. Persistent rumors suggested that he bribed an arms dealer working with the Cuban regime[300] or paid a $1 million ransom to Raul Castro, Fidel Castro's brother[301].

———

While serving a one-year sentence for contempt of court[302], Sam Giancana enjoyed several privileges thanks to bribed guards. He had food and fine Cuban cigars delivered, his laundry done by prison staff, and even permission to leave his cell at night to watch television in another room[303].

———

In 1936, Luciano was sentenced to thirty to fifty years in prison for running a prostitution ring[304]. Seeking a way out, he asked his close associate Albert Anastasia to sabotage the ocean liner *Normandie* while it was docked in New York Harbor in 1942[305]. The U.S. government quickly realized that safeguarding its coasts depended on the mafia, which controlled the dockworkers' union. The authorities reluctantly accepted Luciano's audacious deal: significant sentence reduction in exchange for his complete protection of the docks under his command[306]. The stakes were high—New York ports handled nearly half of America's foreign trade[307]. Without food and supplies crossing the Atlantic, European allies could have faced disaster in World War II. In 1946, Governor Thomas Dewey honored the agreement by releasing Luciano on the condition that he be deported to Italy[308].

In July 1938, two inmates serving life sentences at Alcatraz hatched a plot to kidnap Secretary of the Interior Harold Ickes. They intended to demand a presidential pardon from Roosevelt in exchange for his release. However, the plan fell apart when Al Capone refused to provide the $10,000 needed to fund the operation. The former Chicago boss dismissed the idea, declaring that "President Roosevelt wouldn't free anybody if his whole family was snatched!"[309]

John Gotti paid the Aryan Brotherhood, an ultra-violent Nazi gang, to ensure his protection in prison. He also enlisted their help to murder Walter Johnson, a Black inmate who had struck him in the eye. However, even with a $500,000 payout on the line, the contract was never fulfilled[310].

The Lewisburg federal penitentiary had a dormitory separate from the main building, where incarcerated mobsters lived in comfort[311]. The rooms featured bath oils, wine, silverware, and even a cooler to keep meat and cheeses fresh. Most of the guards were corrupt, smuggling in fine foods for the gangsters—veal chops, shrimp, and lobster were all available to those who could pay. Paul Vario, for instance, spent up to $1,000 a week to maintain total luxury. During his two-and-a-half-year stay, he visited the common dining hall no more than five times[312].

———

As Alcatraz's wealthiest inmate, Al Capone occasionally shared his generosity with fellow prisoners. During the holiday season, he gave Christmas gifts to his unlucky companions, even to those who had tried to kill him[313].

———

While serving time for conspiracy and attempted extortion[314], Joe Gallo occupied himself by devouring books on philosophy. He could read up to eight a day and had a particular fondness for Schopenhauer, Kant, and Voltaire. Determined to remember the most profound thoughts of great thinkers, he filled a notebook with their quotations[315]. He also enjoyed debating these ideas with Nicky Barnes, a fellow inmate and heroin dealer with whom he had befriended[316].

HIGH STAKES

Arnold Rothstein in Chicago in 1919

Arnold Rothstein loved games of chance[317] but hated taking risks. To bet with peace of mind, he didn't hesitate to cheat[318]. "I never played with a man I wasn't sure I could beat" he said unapologetically[319]. For example, he rigged horse races by inserting small sponges into the nostrils of rival horses to hinder their breathing. Even so, his schemes sometimes failed. During an epic poker game that lasted from September 8 to 10, 1928, he indeed lost a staggering $322,000[320].

The famous *Flamingo* hotel-casino in Las Vegas was built with mob money under the supervision of Benjamin Siegel[321]. But before it became one of the city's crown jewels, the establishment—named after the nickname of his girlfriend, Virginia Hill[322]—almost never came to fruition. Initially budgeted at $1 million[323], the project suffered from Siegel's erratic management[324], ballooning to nearly $6 million in just three years[325]. Worse, the grand opening on December 26, 1946, was a resounding failure[326]. Alarmed about their investment, his creditors investigated the *Flamingo*'s accounts. They discovered that $600,000 had been embezzled, and that Virginia Hill had conveniently purchased a house in the upscale town of Lucerne, Switzerland[327]. Whether or not Siegel was aware of the missing money, the mobster had signed his death warrant. On June 20, 1947, Siegel was shot nine times in his Las Vegas home. His left eye was blown four meters from his head, landing on the dining room floor[328].

John Gotti was an avid gambler, particularly fond of card games. Though not very good at poker, he made up for it by wagering money during marathon sessions of Scrabble and Monopoly. He also held his own in chess[329].

Some mobsters were very fond of golf. Despite his penchant for cheating, Sam Giancana had a respectable handicap of fourteen. Eager to improve his technique, he didn't hesitate to take private lessons late into the night. Jack "Machine Gun" McGurn, on the other hand, had a higher skill level and even participated in the Western Open in

1933. Of course, the gangster never forgot to slip a machine gun into his golf bag when practicing, just in case of an unexpected encounter. Al Capone, however, was less impressive on the greens. His putting was poor, and his balls often veered far off the fairway. On one occasion, the gun he kept in his bag accidentally discharged, shooting him in the leg and landing him in the hospital[330].

In 1923, the heavyweight boxing match between star Jack Dempsey and Luis Angel Firpo was a sold-out event. Unable to acquire tickets through legal means, Luciano purchased two hundred seats reserved for the press at $25,000 each. He then shared them with friends and enjoyed the fight as if nothing had happened[331].

Al Capone was a compulsive gambler. He particularly enjoyed craps and betting heavily on horse races. When he won money, he didn't hesitate to throw lavish parties in honor of the jockeys who crossed the finish line in the right order. Unfortunately, Capone could also lose staggering amounts. He once confided to a journalist that he had squandered $7.5 million in less than two years due to gambling[332].

In 1937, Walter Sage, who managed a slot machine operation for the New York Mafia, was murdered with thirty-two icepick stabs for embezzling part of the proceeds. His body was weighted down with a slot machine and submerged in a lake[333].

Before embarking on a criminal career that would eventually make him the head of the Genovese family, Vincent "The Chin" Gigante ruled the boxing ring. A professional boxer from 1944 to 1947, he fought twenty-five matches in the light-heavyweight category, achieving twenty-one victories, including two by knockout. The mobster even performed four times at the iconic *Madison Square Garden*[334], where Marilyn Monroe would later sing her now-famous *Happy Birthday Mr. Pre-*

sident for John F. Kennedy's birthday in front of more than fifteen thousand people[335].

To circumvent the anti-gambling laws of the 1930s in the United States, Frank Costello's slot machines rewarded players with mint candies. The sweets, dispensed if three cherries or lemons appeared on the reels, could then be exchanged for cash. Naturally, this legal loophole was tenuous, and Costello generously bribed politicians and law enforcement to protect his operation[336]. With five thousand machines spread across New York City, the mobster raked in nearly $50,000 a day[337]. A few years later, however, Mayor Fiorello La Guardia dismantled his network, personally smashing several machines with a sledgehammer and tossing them into the water as journalists captured the scene[338].

Arnold Rothstein was a master pool player[339]. He could engage in marathon matches lasting up to thirty-two hours and had no qualms about wagering thousands of dollars on his victories[340].

Shortly after regaining control of Cuba via his 1952 coup d'état, Fulgencio Batista appointed Meyer Lansky as his gambling advisor, granting him an annual salary of $25,000 (equivalent to roughly $295,000 in 2025). Leveraging the support of a corrupt regime determined to turn Havana into a gambler's paradise[341], the mobster oversaw the construction of luxury hotel-casinos such as the *Sevilla Biltmore*, the *Havana Hilton*, and the *Hotel Nacional*. Naturally, Lansky invited his American Mafia associates to partake in the profits. Families like the Luccheses and Trafficantes poured dirty money into the island[342], benefiting from Batista's generous incentives, including tax exemptions, duty-free imports, and even public subsidies[343]. In return, Batista received hefty bribes from his partners, allowing him to flee Cuba with nearly $300 million stashed in offshore accounts when Fidel Castro ousted him in 1958[344].

The Lucchese family dominated the boxing world from the 1940s to the 1960s. With mobster Frankie "Mr. Gray" Carbo at the helm, they controlled fight lineups and often predetermined outcomes, reaping massive profits from risk-free bets. Boxer Jake LaMotta, who inspired the film *Raging Bull*, admitted to throwing his 1947 fight against Billy Fox under Carbo's orders[345]: "By then, if there was anybody in the Garden who didn't know what was happening he must have been dead drunk."[346]

Benjamin Siegel reportedly wagered up to $15,000 a day on horse races, telling tax inspectors that gambling was his sole source of income[347].

A study by the New York Police Department's Organized Crime Control Bureau estimated that mafia-controlled betting agencies raked in over $1 billion during each Super Bowl in the 1990s. By collecting a fifteen percent commission on wagers, New York's Five Families earned an impressive profit of approximately $150 million in a single evening[348].

SWING TIME

Frank Sinatra posing with Carlo Gambino (third right) and
Paul Castellano (first left), 1976

Jazz pianist Fats Waller was kidnapped by four mobsters while performing at Chicago's *Sherman Hotel*. Forced into a limousine at gunpoint, he was taken to Al Capone's headquarters, where he was compelled to play for three days straight to properly celebrate the infamous gangster's birthday[349]. Despite the stressful situation, Waller entertained the crowd and was regularly rewarded with $100 bills stuffed into his pockets. Once released, he remarked that the ordeal was unforgettable, as it was the first time he had ever drunk champagne[350].

Anthony Sinatra, father of Frank Sinatra, lived on the same street as Lucky Luciano in Lercara Friddi, Sicily: Via Margherita di Savoia[351]. After immigrating to the United States, Anthony started boxing under the Irish alias Marty O'Brien to boost his credibility and the betting on his fights[352]. Years later, he used the initials of his pseudonym to name a bar: the *MOB*[353]. A humorous choice, given that "mob" is American slang for the Mafia. The bar attracted several mobsters[354], including Vincent "Jimmy Blue Eyes" Alo, who once said: "I knew Frank Sinatra from when he was a kid. He always wanted to be a gangster, this phony bastard."[355]

Alphonse "Little Al" D'Arco gave his lawyer George Spitz $8,000 to buy musical instruments for his children[356]. The results exceeded all expectations. The younger son, Dan Spitz, went on to found the heavy metal band Anthrax, selling over ten million albums worldwide[357] and earning six Grammy nominations along the way[358]. The elder son contributed to two albums by the iconic rock band Black Sabbath[359].

Bob Dylan caused a scandal with the release of his 1976 album *Desire* because of the song *Joey*, an eleven-minute ballad praising Joe Gallo[360]. Despite Gallo's history as a hitman for the Profaci family and his prison sentence for extortion, the lyrics were full of sympathy for him[361]:

> *They got him on conspiracy, they were never sure who with.*
> *(…)*
> *They threw him in the hole one time for tryin' to stop a strike*
> *His closest friends were black men 'cause they seemed to understand*
> *What it's like to be in society with a shackle on your hand.*
> *(…)*
> *He dressed like Jimmy Cagney and I swear he did look great.*
> *(…)*
> *And someday if God's in heaven overlookin' his preserve*
> *I know the men that shot him down will get what they deserve*[362].

The controversy didn't stop the album from selling nearly three million copies[363].

An opera enthusiast, Big Jim Colosimo was friends with the Italian tenor Enrico Caruso, who frequently dined at his Chicago restaurant. While the establishment couldn't compete with the grandeur of London's *Royal Opera House* or Milan's *La Scala*, *Colosimo's Café* was a hotspot for the city's elite. Patrons were drawn to its mahogany bar and green velvet walls adorned with gold filigree[364].

The opera Michael Corleone attends at the end of *The Godfather Part III* is *Cavalleria Rusticana*[365], composed by Pietro Mascagni in 1890. The story tells the tragic fate of a man who discovers his fiancée has married someone else while he was away at war[366]. The parallel with the film's plot is intriguing, as Michael Corleone's journey begins at his sister's wedding, where he returns as a decorated World War II hero.

In 1946, Joe Adonis stumbled upon a black-market recording of a farting contest[367]. Amused, he tasked Harold Conrad, a press agent[368] for a casino in which he had a stake[369], with purchasing fifty-two copies at $4 each. Adonis then instructed Conrad to sell them to the casino's patrons for $50 apiece, netting a tidy profit of $2,392[370].

At John F. Kennedy's father's request, Sinatra introduced the Kennedy family to the Chicago mob, then led by Sam Giancana. Ahead of the 1960 Democratic primaries and presidential election, the Kennedys sought to secure union votes controlled by the mafia[371]. Giancana, in turn, saw the connection as a gateway to influence within the White House. But after winning the election, Kennedy betrayed Giancana by unleashing a relentless crackdown on organized crime through his brother, Attorney General Bobby Kennedy. The crackdown resulted in the imprisonment of over a hundred mobsters[372]. Furious and holding Sinatra accountable for the toxic alliance, Giancana sent a decapitated sheep's head to Sinatra's Florida hotel room[373]. Fully grasping the warning, Sinatra kept his mouth shut and performed free or heavily discounted shows at mob-controlled casinos to make amends[374].

Despite the mafia's grip on jazz clubs, many musicians appreciated gangsters for providing performance opportunities[375], paying on time, and ensuring their safety[376]. Legendary trumpeter Louis Armstrong openly admitted preferring to play at venues tied to organized crime. From the start of his career, he was supported by Henri Matranga, a New Orleans mob boss who regularly hired him for gigs[377] and bribed judges to keep him out of jail[378]. Later, Armstrong continued his risky associations as the star performer at the *Sunset Café*, one of Al Capone's clubs in Chicago[379].

In 1927, jazz singer Joe E. Lewis decided not to renew his contract with the *Green Mill Garden*, one of Al Capone's Chicago clubs, opting instead for a higher salary at the *New Rendezvous*[380]. Furious over the news, Capone's lieutenant Jack "Machine Gun" McGurn threatened him with serious consequences if he left[381]. Undeterred, Lewis went through with the move and found great success at the *New Rendezvous*[382]. In retaliation, three gangsters broke into his hotel room[383] and slashed his vocal cords[384]. Miraculously, the jazzman was able to resume his career after two long years of recovery[385].

Harry Cohn, head of Columbia Pictures, couldn't stand that the studio star Kim Novak was dating the African-American singer Sammy Davis Jr. Upon learning of their relationship, Cohn even had a heart attack[386]. Determined to end the romance, Cohn enlisted the mafia to threaten Davis, warning that they would gouge out his remaining eye if he didn't immediately marry another woman[387]. Already blind in one eye and terrified of losing his sight entirely, Davis broke off the relationship with Novak and married backup singer Loray White a few days later[388].

In 1947, Frank Sinatra was allegedly spotted at several private parties in Havana alongside Lucky Luciano and other top mafia figures. An FBI report even mentioned orgies involving prostitutes[389]. Although the crooner claimed to know nothing of the gangster's background, a raid on

Luciano's Rome apartment later uncovered a silver cigarette case engraved with the inscription: "To my dear pal Lucky, from his friend, Frank Sinatra."[390]

———

Al Capone was a great opera lover. He particularly enjoyed listening to Giuseppe Verdi and Enrico Caruso, and could even read their musical scores[391]. When he was imprisoned in Alcatraz, however, the boss of the Outfit radically changed his tune for the banjo, which he played every weekend in the shower[392]. He even managed to set up a small orchestra by buying instruments for prisoners who could not afford them[393]. Blessed with a good ear, he also composed an Italian ballad titled *Madonna Mia* in honor of his wife Mae during his incarceration. Rediscovered in 2009, the song was put up for sale by a Boston archivist for $65,000[394].

———

Hot Chocolates, the musical revue that marked Louis Armstrong's Broadway debut in 1929, was bankrolled by Arnold Rothstein[395] and Dutch Schultz[396]. The show enjoyed notable success, with two hundred and nineteen performances[397]. Yet, the production's journey was anything but smooth. Schutz indeed did not hesitate to impose his artistic choices on the composer Andy Razaf by threatening him with a pistol to his temple[398].

In 1969, Mario Puzo, author of *The Godfather*, attempted to greet Frank Sinatra at *Chasen's* restaurant in Los Angeles. Far from receiving the warm exchange he had hoped for, Puzo was insulted by the singer, who even threatened to break his legs. Sinatra detested being associated with the character of Johnny Fontane, a singer in decline who relied on Don Corleone's help to land a movie role. While Fontane was entirely fictional, the parallels with Sinatra's career, depending on perspective, were hard to ignore[399].

To celebrate the opening of the *Colonial Inn*, his new casino in Hallandale, Florida, Meyer Lansky hired singer Carmen Miranda. But the "Brazilian Bombshell," as her fans called her, was unimpressed with the maracas provided by the venue. The mobster had no choice but to make a last-minute trip to Havana to buy models that suited her, salvaging the evening[400].

In 1956, crooner Tony Bennett performed at the wedding of Joseph Bonanno's son to Joe Profaci's daughter[401]. The lavish reception took place at the upscale *Astor Hotel* in New York, with over three thousand prominent guests, including celebrities[402], a member of Congress[403], and most of the mafia's top brass[404].

When Frank Sinatra refused to sing for the Italian-American Anti-Defamation League in November 1971, Joe Colombo, head of the Colombo family and founder of the organization, put a contract on his life. "[Sinatra] called me every day crying" Vincent "Jimmy Blue Eyes" Alo later said. Terrified by the threats, the crooner quickly changed his mind and took the stage, much to Colombo's delight[405].

When FBI agent Jeffrey Sallet went to arrest Joey Massino at his home on January 9, 2003[406], he was listening to *No Sleep Till Brooklyn* by the Beastie Boys[407]. A fitting soundtrack for the Bonanno family boss, who spent a long day at FBI headquarters before being sent to court in… Brooklyn[408].

HOLLYWOOD & FICTION

Benjamin "Bugsy" Siegel in 1944

A year before the release of his book *The Godfather*, Mario Puzo was $20,000 in debt, partly due to his gambling problems[409]. Luckily for his finances, the novel sold twenty-one million copies worldwide[410] and brought Don Corleone's saga to Hollywood with Francis Ford Coppola's 1972 adaptation[411]. Mobsters loved the story so much that they adopted the term "godfather" coined by Puzo, and revived old customs like kissing the boss's ring as a sign of respect[412].

Anthony "Tough Tony" Anastasio, who controlled Brooklyn's docks for the Gambino family, threatened to block shipments from cigarette maker L&M if they continued funding ABC's series *The Untouchables*. Indeed, the mafia wasn't pleased with Italian characters being portrayed as the villains[413].

In the 1930s, many Hollywood unions were under mafia control. Benjamin "Bugsy" Siegel, for example, dominated the extras' guild. Under his rule, studios couldn't hire non-members for any scenes. The gangster took a hefty cut from members' wages while extorting producers with threats of strikes that could halt productions. He also demanded that each film hire "phantom" actors to pad his earnings, which totaled $400,000 a year from this union alone[414]. The IATSE, the theatrical technicians' union, wasn't spared either. Two percent of every member's income was siphoned off by their "protectors"[415] while thugs threatened projectionists and stagehands who resisted joining the organization[416]. Even stars and producers were blackmailed over their drinking habits or sexual escapades[417]. Theater owners, meanwhile, faced extortion to end sudden strike actions[418]. Almost no one escaped the mob's net.

In *The Great Gatsby* by F. Scott Fitzgerald, the enigmatic character Wolfsheim, who helped Jay Gatsby amass his fortune, is based on Arnold Rothstein.

> *- Meyer Wolfshiem? No, he's a gambler.*
> *Gatsby hesitated, then added coolly: "He's the man who fixed the World Series in 1919."*[419]

In these lines, Fitzgerald makes a thinly veiled reference to the grave accusations against Rothstein: that he rigged the 1919 American baseball championship to win a colossal sum[420]. Rothstein was never convicted due to a lack of evidence. As a final nod, the author further emphasized this cryptic dialogue:

> - *Why isn't he in jail?*
> - *They can't get him, old sport. He's a smart man*[421].

It is worth noting that Fitzgerald met Rothstein in person, as confirmed by a letter he sent to humorist Corey Ford in 1937: "I'm always starting from the small focal point that impressed me—my own meeting with Arnold Rothstein for instance."[422]

Poet William S. Burroughs drew inspiration from the gibberish Dutch Schultz uttered on his deathbed to write *The Last Words of Dutch Schultz* in 1970[423]. After being shot in the restrooms of the *Palace Chop House*[424], Schultz agonized in the hospital for over twenty hours[425]. Under the influence of drugs to ease the pain[426], the mobster rambled incoherently, dashing the police's hopes of extracting any useful information[427].

Jimmy Hoffa, head of the American Teamsters union, shut down production of the film *The Enemy Within*. The screenplay, which had Paul Newman eyed for the lead role, depicted Justice Department head Robert Kennedy's fight against organized crime. Given Hoffa's own ties to the mafia[428], he threatened 20th Century Fox with multi-million-dollar lawsuits, successfully killing the project[429].

Many Hollywood celebrities enjoyed the company of mobsters. Actor James Caan, known for his performances in *Misery*, *The Yards*, and *The Godfather*, maintained close ties with the underworld. For example, he offered to mortgage his house to pay the bail of a Los Angeles gangster on trial for drug trafficking, and even asked a mobster to "take care" of actor Joe Pesci because of an unpaid debt[430]. Caan was also seen kissing Carmine "The Snake" Persico, boss of the Colombo crime family, while testifying as a witness at a gangster's trial[431]. Benjamin "Bugsy" Siegel also mingled with numerous stars, including George Raft, Jean Harlow, Clark Gable, and Bruce Cabot[432]. Henry Hill, a Lucchese family mobster portrayed by Ray Liotta in Martin Scorsese's *Goodfellas*, summed up these dangerous liaisons perfectly: "All the movie people want to schmooze the hoods. (…) The hoods are like some prized piece of jewelry you parade around with at a party[433]. (…) On the surface, this world seems about as far away from the gangster life as you can imagine. (…) But the slime just below the surface is sickening. (…) It recently occurred to me that my adventures on Pine Street, in Brooklyn, New York, prepared me nicely for swimming with the sharks on Wilshire."[434]

Benjamin Siegel threatened actor Errol Flynn with being cemented into the Sacramento River if he refused to give him twenty-five percent of his fee for the film *The Adventures of Robin Hood*[435]. Flynn quickly complied without resistance[436]. He could console himself, however, as the production went on to win three Oscars in the categories of Best Art Direction, Best Film Editing, and Best Music[437].

Salvatore Maranzano and Joseph Bonanno shared a common interest in cinema. The two mobsters often went to the movies together, particularly enjoying westerns, Maranzano's favorite genre[438]. Bonanno even attended evening acting classes[439]. But although his teacher recognized his talent, he eventually abandoned his training to focus on his illegal activities[440].

Terence Winter, writer and executive producer of HBO's *The Sopranos*, revealed that several mobsters were convinced one of their own was leaking information to the show's production team. Winter learned this surprising anecdote from an FBI agent tasked with analyzing recordings of wiretapped gangsters. The show was indeed so realistic that it created an atmosphere of intense suspicion within mafia circles[441].

Joe Colombo forced Paramount to remove the terms "Mafia" and "Cosa Nostra" from the script of *The Godfather* by threatening to sabotage the film's production. The words were replaced with "family" and "syndicate," respectively. Several of Colombo's associates were also hired as extras by the production[442].

Gregory Scarpa Sr.'s favorite television show was *Mission Impossible*. The mobster even fancied himself as a James Bond-like figure with a license to kill[443].

Joey Massino owned a small restaurant dedicated to the film *Casablanca*. Aptly named *Casa Blanca*, the establishment greeted patrons with a life-sized statue of actor Humphrey Bogart near the entrance hall. The walls were adorned with posters of the film and photographs of its star-studded cast, while the restroom doors were marked by portraits of the two leads, Bogart and Ingrid Bergman[444]. Though the story of the triple Oscar-winning masterpiece[445] is set in Morocco, the menu stayed true to the mafia's roots by prominently featuring Sicilian dishes[446].

New York Police Department detectives Louis Eppolito and Stephen Caracappa secretly served as informants for Anthony "Gaspipe" Casso from 1986 to 1993. The Lucchese family underboss paid them $4,000 a month for their services and even entrusted them with several murder contracts, offering bonuses of up to $75,000. The corrupt officers were convicted of eight murders, two attempted homicides, obstruction of justice, drug trafficking, money laundering, and leaking sensitive information to the mafia[447]. Before being sentenced to life in prison for his crimes[448], Eppolito had a more honorable claim to fame: a side career as a Hollywood actor. He appeared in two TV movies and thirteen feature films, including *Goodfellas* and *Predator 2*[449].

BAGATELLE

Vito Genovese, photographed by the World Telegram

Vito Genovese ordered the execution of the husband of the woman he desired. The unfortunate man was strangled and left for the pigeons on a Manhattan rooftop[450]. Two weeks later, the gangster finally married his beloved[451]. However, the marital bliss was short-lived. In 1953, his wife filed for divorce and testified against him in court, accusing him of racketeering, drug trafficking, and even fraternizing with Nazi leader Hermann Göring during a trip to Italy[452].

After suffering heavy financial losses from unlucky horse racing bets, Arnold Rothstein pawned his future wife's engagement ring. It took him six months to buy it back[453].

The wife of Judge John Foster Symes regularly performed stripteases at the *Moonlight Ranch*, a jazz club in Denver controlled by the mob. When the establishment was busted for illegal alcohol sales, it was ironically Symes who presided over the trial. He relished the opportunity to deliver justice, declaring the *Moonlight Ranch* "a stench in the nostrils of decent and respectable citizens."[454]

The pornographic film *Deep Throat* was financed by Anthony Peraino, a mobster from the Colombo family, for $22,000[455]. Since the gangster didn't want Linda Lovelace in the lead role, the actress's boyfriend, who feared she'd lose her fee, forced her to perform daily fellatio on Peraino[456]. Ultimately, Lovelace kept her part, and the film became a global success. By some estimates, it grossed up to $600 million[457]—a return on investment of more than two million percent.

Benjamin Siegel was arrested for rape on January 26, 1926. However, the charges were dropped after the unexpected disappearance of his accuser. Siegel would later claim that his alleged victim had a change of heart, saying he was the best lover she'd ever had[458].

Big Jim Colosimo earned more than $50,000 a month from his brothels. His commission was $1.20 out of the $2.00 that each girl made per client[459]. An amateur of prostitutes, he eventually married Victoria Moresco, the madam of a gentlemen's club[460].

James T. Ellison, leader of the notorious Gopher Gang that controlled Manhattan until 1910, was openly homosexual and founded one of New York's first gay bars, the *Paresis*. After his conviction for murder in 1911, he developed mental health issues and spent the remainder of his life confined to a psychiatric institution[461].

Thomas Eboli, acting boss of the Genovese family, was executed on July 16, 1972, for failing to repay $4 million to Carlo Gambino[462]. Out of respect for his status, the hitmen assigned to the contract waited until he left his mistress's apartment in Brooklyn before riddling him with bullets[463].

―――

Mafia families prohibited their members from performing cunnilingus. According to Salvatore Vitale, a Bonanno family captain turned government informant, an associate was denied full membership after he was overheard discussing the act[464].

―――

Paul Castellano seduced his Colombian housekeeper using a computer. Initially hired with limited English skills, the employee relied on the device to translate his instructions into Spanish. Over time, the boss's commands gradually evolved into affectionate messages[465]. Surprisingly, this avant-garde courting method worked, as Castellano spent the rest of his days with his beloved in his Staten Island mansion[466].

―――

From New York's Sing Sing prison, the Italian mafia sent denunciatory letters to the families of gangsters suspected of engaging in homosexual activities. Even a casual conversation with an inmate believed to be gay could serve as evidence[467].

———

While serving a one-hundred and thirty-nine year sentence at the federal prison in Lompoc, Carmine Persico bribed guards to allow him to sleep with a lawyer who visited him regularly[468]. Between these romantic interludes, the Colombo family boss passed the time by playing drums in a band composed of two gangsters and a heroin trafficker. He also managed a cultural club dedicated to Italian heritage, which he had founded[469].

———

Anthony "Gaspipe" Casso had an unusual approach to neighborly relations. When one of his neighbors complained about a persistent suitor pursuing his daughter, the Lucchese family underboss stepped in by sending a hitman to punish the apprentice Don Juan. The victim's body was discovered on December 7, 1988, in a car in Brooklyn[470].

BUON APPETITO

Sam Giancana, boss of the Chicago Outfit

Anthony Casso, underboss of the Lucchese family, enjoyed flaunting his wealth at restaurants. During a meal at Miami's upscale *Forge*, he ordered their most expensive bottle of wine, priced at nearly ten thousand dollars. Once served, he asked for a cola and poured it into his wine glass. The sommelier nearly fainted at the sight[471].

Joey Massino was an excellent cook. When he wasn't busy running the Bonanno family, one of his favorite pastimes was creating and testing new recipes[472]. However, his indulgence in food caused him to gain significant weight, eventually reaching four hundred pounds[473]. When FBI undercover agent Joseph Pistone testified against Massino in court, the mobster asked who would play his role in the film *Donnie Brasco*. Pistone quipped that the production was struggling to find an actor fat enough for the part[474].

During FBI surveillance of Meyer Lansky's room at New York's *Volney Hotel* in 1962, federal agents discovered that his diet largely consisted of sardines, Jell-O, Irish lamb stew, and ham[475].

During Prohibition, the U.S. government ordered the poisoning of legal industrial spirits, which were sometimes used by bootleggers to build up their supplies. The goal was to discourage people from taking risks by going to speakeasies[476]. Seymour M. Lowman, Assistant Secretary of the Treasury, even declared that if the result was a sober America, "a good job will have been done." But far from having the desired effect, the measure dramatically increased the number of cases of blindness and deaths among drinkers[477]. It is estimated that about fifty thousand people died from drinking contaminated whiskey between 1920 and 1933[478].

Arnold Rothstein conducted most of his operations at *Lindy's* restaurant in Times Square. He spent so much time at his table that patrons often assumed he was the owner of the establishment[479].

Enoch "Nucky" Johnson had the habit of eating breakfast at three in the afternoon after being massaged with soothing balms and essential oils by his valet[480]. From his ninth-floor suite at the *Ritz-Carlton*, facing the ocean, he would enjoy freshly squeezed orange juice, six eggs, and a ham steak[481].

During Prohibition, New York City had nearly thirty-two thousand speakeasies[482]. By comparison, the city had only two thousand one hundred licensed bars in 2018[483].

Many mafiosi were murdered in a restaurant. Here are a few examples:

- "Crazy" Joe Gallo, on April 7, 1972, at the *Umbertos Clam House* in Little Italy. Gallo was celebrating his forty-third birthday with his wife, daughter, sister and bodyguard "Pete The Greek." As a gift, four killers entered the establishment and shot him twenty times[484]. The mastermind behind the hit remains unknown.

- Joe "The Boss" Masseria, on April 15, 1931, at *Nuova Villa Tammaro*, a seafood spot in Coney Island. Lucky Luciano orchestrated the murder after playing cards at his table. Shortly after slipping away to the bathroom, Luciano sent four killers to end the gangster's reign[485]. Lying on the floor, Masseria's lifeless hand held an ace of spades[486].

- Carmine Galante, unofficial boss of the Bonanno family, on July 12, 1979, in the patio of *Joe and Mary's Italian-American Restaurant* in Brooklyn. At 2:45 p.m., as he waited for coffee with his two bodyguards, a dealer, and the restaurant's owner, three assassins in ski masks burst in and killed him. Galante died with his signature cigar still in his mouth[487].

- Paul Castellano, head of the Gambino family, outside the *Sparks Steak House* in Manhattan on December 16, 1985. Barely out of their limousine, Castellano and his captain Thomas

Bilotti were gunned down by three men with automatic rifles[488]. The hit was ordered by John Gotti, who watched the spectacle from his car, parked a few feet away[489]. A few weeks later, Gotti officially took over as head of the Gambino family[490].

- Dutch Schultz, on October 23, 1935, at the *Palace Chop House and Tavern* in Newark. Schultz's fate was sealed by the mafia bosses, who feared his plan to assassinate prosecutor Thomas E. Dewey would draw unwanted attention[491]. He was fatally shot in the restroom[492].

- Willie Moretti, on October 4, 1951, at *Joe's Elbow Room Restaurant* in Cliffside Park. Suffering cognitive decline from syphilis, Moretti was killed to prevent him from talking too much[493]. Former mobster-turned-government witness Joe Valachi described it as "a mercy killing, as he was sick."[494]

- Big Jim Colosimo, on May 11, 1920, in his own restaurant, *Colosimo's Café*, at 2128 South Wabash in Chicago[495]. The killer's identity remains unconfirmed, though suspicion points to his captain, Johnny Torrio, who wanted to expand the family's operations into bootlegging—a plan Colosimo opposed[496].

Joe "The Boss" Masseria was also nicknamed "The Glutton" for his poor table manners and voracious appetite. He could easily devour three plates of pasta alongside his main course, spraying his dining companions with food as he spoke[497]. Joseph Bonanno remarked that Masseria ate "as if he were a drooling mastiff" and "had the table manners of a Hun" when enjoying a dish[498].

The stills of New York's top bootleggers could produce up to a hundred gallons of alcohol daily at a ridiculously low cost of fifty cents per gallon, which sold for around $12. Drawn to the lucrative trade, unscrupulous citizens made their own alcohol from corn sugar, beets, or fermented potato peels. After filling a few bottles, they diluted the contents with water. Unfortunately, since kitchen sinks of the era were often too small, amateur bootleggers resorted to using their bathtub faucets. To mask the foul taste of this "bathtub gin," speakeasy bartenders often mixed it with bitters or fruit juices, giving rise to many classic cocktails[499].

Frank Costello had a habit of rising at five in the morning to enjoy breakfast with the *New York Times*[500]. His meal consisted of a cup of black coffee with no sugar and a slice of toast spread with margarine[501].

Although he violated most of the Bible's commandments, Sam Giancana insisted that his wife say grace before anyone touched the food on the table. He also observed other Catholic traditions, such as abstaining from meat on Fridays and Christmas Eve[502]. These culinary rituals, however, did not bring him luck. The boss of the Outfit was indeed assassinated with seven bullets to the neck and head[503] while cooking a dish of sausage and spinach in the basement of his home[504].

Vincent Mangano, boss of the Mangano family, regularly hosted his friends Joe Profaci and Joseph Bonanno for endless banquets at his ranch or New York home[505]. Mangano personally prepared fish, veal, filet mignon, and, of course, pasta to satisfy his distinguished guests[506]. Between plates, the heads of the most powerful criminal families in the United States would sing and toast while reciting improvised Sicilian poems[507].

After assassinating Cesare Bonventre, a lieutenant in the Bonanno family, the killers sent by boss Joey Massino[508] tried to dispose of his body by feeding it into a meat grinder. Unfortunately, the machine jammed after reducing the gangster's torso into small pieces. The apprentice butchers had to finish the job by hiding the remaining body parts into three glue barrels[509].

―――

Enoch "Nucky" Johnson loved salt water taffy. These delightful treats were invented by one of his fellow Atlantic City residents, David Bradley[510].

―――

The Genovese family controlled the sale and distribution of fish in New York, holding thousands of restaurateurs and storekeepers at their mercy. Deliveries were subject to payment of a tax[511], and the rare customers who dared to protest had their tires slashed, were beaten up or even threatened with death. But this racket, which brought in around three million dollars a year, was less lucrative than the revenue generated by the "protection" fees charged to retailers selling their seafood. With one hundred and fifty million pounds of fish sold each year, the market was worth nearly a billion dollars[512].

BIBLIOGRAPHY

Agent Joseph Pistone as Donnie Brasco

67 BOOKS

- Boardwalk Empire: The Birth, High Times, and Corruption of Atlantic City, Nelson Johnson
- Boss of Bosses: The Fall of the Godfather, the FBI and Paul Castellano, Joseph F. O'Brien et Andris Kurins
- Bringing Down the Mob: The War Against the American Mafia, Thomas Reppetto
- Brutal: The Untold Story of My Life Inside Whitey Bulger's Irish Mob, Kevin Weeks
- Capone: The Man and the Era, Laurence Bergreen
- Capone, John Kobler
- Cigar City Mafia: A Complete History of the Tampa Underworld, Scott Deitche
- Corruption in Cuba: Castro and Beyond, Sergio Díaz-Briquets et Jorge Pérez-López
- Cosa Nostra, un Siècle d'Histoire, Eric Frattini
- Crime, Justice, and Society, Calvin J. Larson et Gerald R. Garrett
- Deal With The Devil: The FBI's Secret Thirty-Year Relationship With a Mafia Killer, Peter Lance
- Donnie Brasco: My Undercover Life in the Mafia, Joseph D. Pistone

- Donnie Brasco: Unfinished Business, Joseph D. Pistone
- Fats Waller, Maurice Waller et Anthony Calabrese
- Five Families: The Rise, Decline, and Resurgence of America's Most Powerful Mafia Empires, Selwyn Raab
- For the Sins of My Father: A Mafia Killer, His Son, and the Legacy of a Mob Life, Albert DeMeo
- Frank Sinatra, une Mythologie Américaine, Steven Jezo-Vannier
- Gangsters and Goodfellas: The Mob, Witness Protection, and Life on the Run, Henry Hill
- Goddess: The Secret Lives of Marilyn Monroe, Anthony Summers
- Gotti, Jerry Capeci et Gene Mustain
- Homme d'Honneur, Joseph Bonanno
- Iced: The Story of Organized Crime in Canada, Stephen Schneider
- J.E. Hoover Confidential, Anthony Summers
- Jazz and the Underworld: Dangerous Rhythms, T.J. English
- Journal of Law and Criminology, Rackets in America, volume 49, Virgil W. Peterson

- Kill the Dutchman!: The Story of Dutch Schultz, Paul Sann
- King of the Godfathers: "Big Joey" Massino and the Fall of the Bonanno Crime Family, Anthony M. Destefano
- La Mafia à Hollywood, Tim Adler
- Les Affranchis: La Vie Quotidienne dans la Mafia, Nicholas Pileggi
- Le Syndicat du Crime, Jean-Michel Charlier
- Les Secrets de la Mafia, Philippe Di Folco
- Little Man: Meyer Lansky and the Gangster Life, Robert Lacey
- Mafia Princess: Growing Up in Sam Giancana's Family, Antoinette Giancana et Thomas C. Renner
- Mickey Cohen: The Life and Crimes of L.A.'s Notorious Mobster, Tere Tereba
- Mob Boss: The Life of Little Al D'Arco, the Man Who Brought Down the Mafia, Jerry Capeci et Tom Robbins
- Mob Lawyer, Frank Ragano et Selwyn Raab
- Mob Star, Jerry Capeci et Gene Mustain
- Mobsters and Thugs: Quotes From the Underworld, Olindo Romeo Chiocca
- Mr. Capone, Robert J. Schoenberg

- Murder Machine: A True Story of Murder, Madness and The Mafia, Gene Mustain et Jerry Capeci
- Olives: The Life and Lore of a Noble Fruit, Mort Rosenbaum
- On the Rock: Twenty-Five Years in Alcatraz, Alvin Karpis
- Oncle Frank: Frank Costello, Vie et Mort d'un Parrain, Leonard Katz
- Project MKULTRA, the CIA's Program of Research in Behavioral Modification, U.S. Government
- Raging Bull: My Story, Jack La Motta, Joseph Carter et Peter Savage
- Rothstein: The Life, Times, and Murder of the Criminal Genius Who Fixed the 1919 World Series, David Pietrusza
- Sinatra: The Life, Anthony Summers
- Smartest Bandit of the Cookson Hills, Carl Janaway
- The Bob Dylan Albums: A Critical Study, Anthony Varesi
- The Complete Idiot's Guide to the Mafia, Jerry Capeci

- The Encyclopedia of Unsolved Crimes, Michael Newton
- The Federal Bureau of Investigation: History, Powers, and Controversies of the FBI, Douglas M. Charles et Aaaron J. Stockham
- The Godfather Effect: Changing Hollywood, America, and Me, Tom Santopietro
- The Great Gatsby, Francis Scott Fitzgerald
- The Hoffa Wars: The Rise and Fall of Jimmy Hoffa, Dan E. Moldea
- The Last Godfather: The Rise and Fall of Joey Massino, Simon Crittle
- The Mad Ones: Crazy Joe Gallo and the Revolution at the Edge of the Underworld, Tom Folsom
- The Mafia at War, Allied Collusion With the Mob, Tim Newark
- The Mafia Encyclopedia, Carl Sifakis
- The Origin of Organized Crime in America: The New York City Mafia, 1891-1931, David Critchley
- The Sinatra Club: My Life Inside the New York Mafia, Salvatore Polisi
- The Valachi Papers, Peter Maas
- The Way of the Wiseguy, Joseph D. Pistone
- Tommy Gun: How General Thompson's Submachine Gun Wrote History, Bill Yenne

- Underboss: Sammy the Bull Gravano's Story of Life in the Mafia, Peter Maas
- We Only Kill Each Other: The Life and Bad Times of Bugsy Siegel, Dean Southern Jennings
- Whitey Bulger: America's Most Wanted Gangster and The Manhunt That Brought Him To Justice, Kevin Cullen

17 NEWSPAPERS AND DOCUMENTS

- Chicago Sunday Tribune
- Chicago Tribune
- Criminal Rico: A Manual For Federal Prosecutors, U.S. Department of Justice
- Fortune
- Golf Chicago Magazine
- Jewish Telegraphic Agency
- Library of Congress
- Los Angeles Times
- New York Daily News
- New York Times
- News-Press, Fort Myers
- The Californian
- The Evening Times
- The United States Attorney's Office, Eastern District of New York

- Time
- United States District Court, Eastern District of New York
- Vanderbilt Law Review

2 NEWS CHANNELS

- C-SPAN
- NBC News

30 WEBSITES

- American Baseball Hall of fame - baseballhall.org
- American Congress - constitution.congress.gov-
- American Government archives - archives.gov
- American Senate - senate.gov
- American Supreme Court - supreme.justia.com
- Best Selling Albums - bestsellingalbums.org
- Black Sabbath - black-sabbath.com
- Bob Dylan - bobdylan.com
- BoxRec - boxrec.com
- Broadway Database - ibdb.com
- Deadline - deadline.com
- Descendant Of Thieves - descendantofthieves.-com
- Find A Grave - findagrave.com
- Getty Images - gettyimages.fr

- Grammy Awards - grammy.com
- Harvard Business School - hbs.edu
- History - historynet.com
- Internet Movie Database - imdb.com
- Justia US Law - law.justia.com
- Last FM - last.fm
- National Library of American Medicine - nlm.nih.gov
- Opera Online - opera-online.com
- Oscars - oscars.org
- Refworld - refworld.org
- Richard Nixon Foundation - nixonfoundation.org
- The Guardian - theguardian.com
- The Mob Museum - themobmuseum.org
- United States Secret Service - secretservice.gov
- Vanity Fair - vanityfair.com
- Winston Churchill - winstonchurchill.org

PHOTO CREDITS

All photographs in this book are copyright-free.

PUBLIC DOMAIN

- Associated Press
- Bernard Gotfryd

- CBS Television
- Federal Bureau of Investigation
- Harris & Ewing
- Joyson Noel
- New York Police Department
- The Evening World
- United States Department of Justice
- US Federal Government
- World Telegram

CREATIVE COMMONS

- Benjamin Siegel: Los Angeles Daily News, Wikimedia
- Enoch Johnson: Brinks38200, Wikimedia

SOURCES

Mugshot of Joe Masseria in 1922

[1] King of the Godfathers: "Big Joey" Massino and the Fall of the Bonanno Crime Family, Anthony M. Destefano, page 72

[2] King of the Godfathers: "Big Joey" Massino and the Fall of the Bonanno Crime Family, Anthony M. Destefano, page 73

[3] We Only Kill Each Other: The Life and Bad Times of Bugsy Siegel, Dean Southern Jennings, page 23

[4] We Only Kill Each Other: The Life and Bad Times of Bugsy Siegel, Dean Southern Jennings, page 50

[5] Whitey Bulger: America's Most Wanted Gangster and The Manhunt That Brought Him To Justice, Kevin Cullen, page 416

[6] Whitey Bulger: America's Most Wanted Gangster and The Manhunt That Brought Him To Justice, Kevin Cullen, page 379

[7] Whitey Bulger: America's Most Wanted Gangster and The Manhunt That Brought Him To Justice, Kevin Cullen, page 411

[8] Whitey Bulger: America's Most Wanted Gangster and The Manhunt That Brought Him To Justice, Kevin Cullen, page 401

[9] Whitey Bulger: America's Most Wanted Gangster and The Manhunt That Brought Him To Justice, Kevin Cullen, page 416

[10] Capone: The Man and the Era, Laurence Bergreen, page 50

[11] Mr. Capone, Robert J. Schoenberg, page 34

[12] Mr. Capone, Robert J. Schoenberg, page 33

[13] Mr. Capone, Robert J. Schoenberg, page 32

[14] Mr. Capone, Robert J. Schoenberg, page 33

[15] Capone, John Kobler, page 15

[16] Capone, John Kobler, page 36

[17] Mr. Capone, Robert J. Schoenberg, page 34

[18] FBI file on Frank Costello, file 62-76543, section 1-2, page 28

[19] Little Man: Meyer Lansky and the Gangster Life, Robert Lacey, page 187

[20] The Mafia Encyclopedia, Carl Sifakis page 10

[21] New York Times, October 26, 1957, page 1

[22] https://themobmuseum.org/

[23] Mobsters and Thugs: Quotes From the Underworld, Olindo Romeo Chiocca, page 58

[24] Capone: The Man and the Era, Laurence Bergreen, page 81

[25] Boardwalk Empire: The Birth, High Times, and Corruption of Atlantic City, Nelson Johnson, page 92

[26] Boardwalk Empire: The Birth, High Times, and Corruption of Atlantic City, Nelson Johnson, page 79

[27] Boardwalk Empire: The Birth, High Times, and Corruption of Atlantic City, Nelson Johnson, page 91

[28] Boardwalk Empire: The Birth, High Times, and Corruption of Atlantic City, Nelson Johnson, page 93

[29] Oncle Frank: Frank Costello, Vie et Mort d'un Parrain, Leonard Katz, page 104

[30] Oncle Frank: Frank Costello, Vie et Mort d'un Parrain, Leonard Katz, page 106

[31] Rothstein: The Life, Times, and Murder of the Criminal Genius Who Fixed the 1919 World Series, David Pietrusza, page 423

[32] Les Secrets de la Mafia, Philippe Di Folco, page 216

[33] Gotti, Jerry Capeci et Gene Mustain, page 159

[34] Mob Star, Jerry Capeci et Gene Mustain, page 11

[35] Gotti, Jerry Capeci et Gene Mustain, page 113

[36] Gotti, Jerry Capeci et Gene Mustain, page 160

[37] https://content.time.com/time/covers/0,16641,19860929,00.html

[38] New York Times, February 19, 1990, page 1

[39] Oncle Frank: Frank Costello, Vie et Mort d'un Parrain, Leonard Katz, page 20

[40] Homme d'Honneur, Joseph Bonanno, page 8

[41] Homme d'Honneur, Joseph Bonanno, page 9

[42] The American Gladiators: Taft Versus Remus, Albert Rosenberg, page 11

[43] The American Gladiators: Taft Versus Remus, Albert Rosenberg, page 116

[44] The American Gladiators: Taft Versus Remus, Albert Rosenberg, page 11

[45] The American Gladiators: Taft Versus Remus, Albert Rosenberg, page 12

[46] We Only Kill Each Other: The Life and Bad Times of Bugsy Siegel, Dean Southern Jennings, page 49

[47] Rothstein: The Life, Times, and Murder of the Criminal Genius Who Fixed the 1919 World Series, David Pietrusza, page 201

[48] Mafia Princess: Growing Up in Sam Giancana's Family, Antoinette Giancana et Thomas C. Renner, page 48

[49] Mafia Princess: Growing Up in Sam Giancana's Family, Antoinette Giancana et Thomas C. Renner, page 49

[50] Mafia Princess: Growing Up in Sam Giancana's Family, Antoinette Giancana et Thomas C. Renner, page 51

[51] Mafia Princess: Growing Up in Sam Giancana's Family, Antoinette Giancana et Thomas C. Renner, page 48

[52] Murder Machine: A True Story of Murder, Madness and The Mafia, Gene Mustain et Jerry Capeci, page 10 of the foreword

[53] For the Sins of My Father: A Mafia Killer, His Son, and the Legacy of a Mob Life, Albert DeMeo, page 67

[54] For the Sins of My Father: A Mafia Killer, His Son, and the Legacy of a Mob Life, Albert DeMeo, page 68

[55] We Only Kill Each Other: The Life and Bad Times of Bugsy Siegel, Dean Southern Jennings, page 81

[56] We Only Kill Each Other: The Life and Bad Times of Bugsy Siegel, Dean Southern Jennings, page 83

[57] We Only Kill Each Other: The Life and Bad Times of Bugsy Siegel, Dean Southern Jennings, page 84

[58] Les Affranchis: La Vie Quotidienne dans la Mafia, Nicholas Pileggi, page 196

[59] Les Affranchis: La Vie Quotidienne dans la Mafia, Nicholas Pileggi, page 197

[60] La Mafia à Hollywood, Tim Adler, page 41

[61] The Way of the Wiseguy, Joseph D. Pistone, page 29

[62] The Way of the Wiseguy, Joseph D. Pistone, page 33

[63] The Way of the Wiseguy, Joseph D. Pistone, page 50

[64] The Way of the Wiseguy, Joseph D. Pistone, page 29

[65] The Way of the Wiseguy, Joseph D. Pistone, page 30

[66] The Way of the Wiseguy, Joseph D. Pistone, page 81

[67] The Way of the Wiseguy, Joseph D. Pistone, page 89

[68] The Way of the Wiseguy, Joseph D. Pistone, page 93

[69] Les Secrets de la Mafia, Philippe Di Folco, page 75

[70] Les Secrets de la Mafia, Philippe Di Folco, page 77

[71] Boardwalk Empire: The Birth, High Times, and Corruption of Atlantic City, Nelson Johnson, page 79

[72] Boardwalk Empire: The Birth, High Times, and Corruption of Atlantic City, Nelson Johnson, page 86

[73] Boardwalk Empire: The Birth, High Times, and Corruption of Atlantic City, Nelson Johnson, page 99

[74] Les Secrets de la Mafia, Philippe Di Folco, page 81

[75] Les Secrets de la Mafia, Philippe Di Folco, page 212

[76] Mob Boss: The Life of Little Al D'Arco, the Man Who Brought Down the Mafia, Jerry Capeci et Tom Robbins, page 122

[77] Homme d'Honneur, Joseph Bonanno, page 206

[78] Homme d'Honneur, Joseph Bonanno, page 153

[79] The Mafia at War, Allied Collusion With the Mob, Tim Newark, page 73

[80] Little Man: Meyer Lansky and the Gangster Life, Robert Lacey, page 16

[81] Little Man: Meyer Lansky and the Gangster Life, Robert Lacey, page 17

[82] The Mafia at War, Allied Collusion With the Mob, Tim Newark, page 73

[83] Organized Crime in Chicago: Beyond the Mafia, Robert M. Lombardo, page 104

[84] The Mafia at War, Allied Collusion With the Mob, Tim Newark, page 116

[85] The Mafia at War, Allied Collusion With the Mob, Tim Newark, page 215

[86] The Mafia at War, Allied Collusion With the Mob, Tim Newark, page 216

[87] The Mafia at War, Allied Collusion With the Mob, Tim Newark, page 226

[88] Mob Boss: The Life of Little Al D'Arco, the Man Who Brought Down the Mafia, Jerry Capeci et Tom Robbins, page 323

[89] Mob Boss: The Life of Little Al D'Arco, the Man Who Brought Down the Mafia, Jerry Capeci et Tom Robbins, page 325

[90] The Californian, October 29, 1984, page 10

[91] Homme d'Honneur, Joseph Bonanno, page 214

[92] New York Times, October 16, 1976, page 28

[93] Les Affranchis: La Vie Quotidienne dans la Mafia, Nicholas Pileggi, page 186

[94] Les Affranchis: La Vie Quotidienne dans la Mafia, Nicholas Pileggi, page 187

[95] Les Affranchis: La Vie Quotidienne dans la Mafia, Nicholas Pileggi, page 188

[96] The Way of the Wiseguy, Joseph D. Pistone, page 110

[97] The Way of the Wiseguy, Joseph D. Pistone, page 111

[98] The Way of the Wiseguy, Joseph D. Pistone, page 112

[99] Les Affranchis: La Vie Quotidienne dans la Mafia, Nicholas Pileggi, page 41

[100] The Federal Bureau of Investigation: History, Powers, and Controversies of the FBI, Douglas M. Charles et Aaaron J. Stockham, page 40

[101] Donnie Brasco: My Undercover Life in the Mafia, Joseph D. Pistone, page 2

[102] We Only Kill Each Other: The Life and Bad Times of Bugsy Siegel, Dean Southern Jennings, page 52

[103] We Only Kill Each Other: The Life and Bad Times of Bugsy Siegel, Dean Southern Jennings, page 53

[104] We Only Kill Each Other: The Life and Bad Times of Bugsy Siegel, Dean Southern Jennings, page 58

[105] Five Families: The Rise, Decline, and Resurgence of America's Most Powerful Mafia Empires, Selwyn Raab, page 336

[106] Underboss: Sammy the Bull Gravano's Story of Life in the Mafia, Peter Maas, page 160

[107] Underboss: Sammy the Bull Gravano's Story of Life in the Mafia, Peter Maas, page 283

[108] Rothstein: The Life, Times, and Murder of the Criminal Genius Who Fixed the 1919 World Series, David Pietrusza, page 1

[109] New York Times, November 7, 1928, page 27

[110] Oncle Frank: Frank Costello, Vie et Mort d'un Parrain, Leonard Katz, page 175

[111] Oncle Frank: Frank Costello, Vie et Mort d'un Parrain, Leonard Katz, page 176

[112] Oncle Frank: Frank Costello, Vie et Mort d'un Parrain, Leonard Katz, page 177

[113] Little Man: Meyer Lansky and the Gangster Life, Robert Lacey, page 211

[114] Five Families: The Rise, Decline, and Resurgence of America's Most Powerful Mafia Empires, Selwyn Raab, page 569

[115] Fortune, November 10, 1986, page 25

[116] New York Times, January 14, 1987, page 1

[117] Underboss: Sammy the Bull Gravano's Story of Life in the Mafia, Peter Maas, page 107

[118] Underboss: Sammy the Bull Gravano's Story of Life in the Mafia, Peter Maas, page 108

[119] https://prohibition.themobmuseum.org/the-history/the-rise-of-organized-crime/the-mob-during-prohibition/

[120] Mr. Capone, Robert J. Schoenberg, page 40

[121] Five Families: The Rise, Decline, and Resurgence of America's Most Powerful Mafia Empires, Selwyn Raab, page 156

[122] Rothstein: The Life, Times, and Murder of the Criminal Genius Who Fixed the 1919 World Series, David Pietrusza, page 4

[123] Rothstein: The Life, Times, and Murder of the Criminal Genius Who Fixed the 1919 World Series, David Pietrusza, page 205

[124] Rothstein: The Life, Times, and Murder of the Criminal Genius Who Fixed the 1919 World Series, David Pietrusza, page 213

[125] Rothstein: The Life, Times, and Murder of the Criminal Genius Who Fixed the 1919 World Series, David Pietrusza, page 195

[126] Rothstein: The Life, Times, and Murder of the Criminal Genius Who Fixed the 1919 World Series, David Pietrusza, page 377

[127] Oncle Frank: Frank Costello, Vie et Mort d'un Parrain, Leonard Katz, page 225

[128] Oncle Frank: Frank Costello, Vie et Mort d'un Parrain, Leonard Katz, page 226

[129] Five Families: The Rise, Decline, and Resurgence of America's Most Powerful Mafia Empires, Selwyn Raab, page 230

[130] Five Families: The Rise, Decline, and Resurgence of America's Most Powerful Mafia Empires, Selwyn Raab, page 285

[131] Five Families: The Rise, Decline, and Resurgence of America's Most Powerful Mafia Empires, Selwyn Raab, page 230

¹³² Oncle Frank: Frank Costello, Vie et Mort d'un Parrain, Leonard Katz, page 143

¹³³ New York Times, January 6, 1973, page 32

¹³⁴ Deal With The Devil: The FBI's Secret Thirty-Year Relationship With a Mafia Killer, Peter Lance, page 29

¹³⁵ Deal With The Devil: The FBI's Secret Thirty-Year Relationship With a Mafia Killer, Peter Lance, page 30

¹³⁶ https://www.historynet.com/two-gun-hart-the-prohibition-cowboy

¹³⁷ Interview with historian Garrett Peck, Library of Congress, October 26, 2011, at 35:56, https://www.loc.gov/item/2021688759

¹³⁸ CIA declassified document https://graphics8.nytimes.com/packages/pdf/national/familyjewels/20070626_ciaandmob.pdf

¹³⁹ American Government Archives https://www.archives.gov/files/research/jfk/releases/2021/docid-32105805.pdf, page 107

¹⁴⁰ Five Families: The Rise, Decline, and Resurgence of America's Most Powerful Mafia Empires, Selwyn Raab, page 3

¹⁴¹ The Valachi Papers, Peter Maas, page 15

¹⁴² Five Families: The Rise, Decline, and Resurgence of America's Most Powerful Mafia Empires, Selwyn Raab, page 4

¹⁴³ Mob Boss: The Life of Little Al D'Arco, the Man Who Brought Down the Mafia, Jerry Capeci et Tom Robbins, page 192

¹⁴⁴ Five Families: The Rise, Decline, and Resurgence of America's Most Powerful Mafia Empires, Selwyn Raab, page 4

[145] Mob Boss: The Life of Little Al D'Arco, the Man Who Brought Down the Mafia, Jerry Capeci et Tom Robbins, page 193

[146] https://www.gov.il/en/departments/policies/government_law_of_return_nativ

[147] Jewish Telegraphic Agency, June 12, 1980, page 3

[148] Little Man: Meyer Lansky and the Gangster Life, Robert Lacey, page 333

[149] Little Man: Meyer Lansky and the Gangster Life, Robert Lacey, page 348

[150] https://www.refworld.org/legal/legislation/natlegbod/1950/en/34127

[151] https://www.senate.gov/about/powers-procedures/investigations/kefauver.htm

[152] https://deadline.com/2016/05/tv-season-2015-2016-series-rankings-shows-full-list-1201763189/

[153] Crime, Justice, and Society, Calvin J. Larson et Gerald R. Garrett, page 152

[154] Gotti, Jerry Capeci et Gene Mustain, page 177

[155] Gotti, Jerry Capeci et Gene Mustain, page 121

[156] Gotti, Jerry Capeci et Gene Mustain, page 122

[157] Gotti, Jerry Capeci et Gene Mustain, page 124

[158] Gotti, Jerry Capeci et Gene Mustain, page 123

[159] New York Times, 7 novembre 1992, page 25

[160] Gotti, Jerry Capeci et Gene Mustain, page 173

[161] The American Gladiators: Taft Versus Remus, Albert Rosenberg, page 3

[162] The American Gladiators: Taft Versus Remus, Albert Rosenberg, page 2

[163] The American Gladiators: Taft Versus Remus, Albert Rosenberg, page 9

[164] The American Gladiators: Taft Versus Remus, Albert Rosenberg, page 13

[165] Interview with historian Bob Batchelor on C-SPAN, September 25, 2019, at 48:50, https://www.c-span.org/video/?464406-1/the-bourbon-king

[166] New York Times, January 21, 1952, page 10

[167] https://winstonchurchill.org/publications/churchill-bulletin/bulletin-163-jan-2022/churchill-style-33/

[168] Tommy Gun: How General Thompson's Submachine Gun Wrote History, Bill Yenne, page 74

[169] Tommy Gun: How General Thompson's Submachine Gun Wrote History, Bill Yenne, page 75

[170] Los Angeles Times, 28 mai 1992, page 25

[171] https://constitution.congress.gov/constitution/amendment-5/

[172] Journal of Law and Criminology, Rackets in America, volume 49, Virgil W. Peterson, page 586

[173] J.E. Hoover Confidential, Anthony Summers, page 221

[174] J.E. Hoover Confidential, Anthony Summers, page 225

[175] J.E. Hoover Confidential, Anthony Summers, page 229

[176] J.E. Hoover Confidential, Anthony Summers, page 89

[177] J.E. Hoover Confidential, Anthony Summers, page 231

[178] J.E. Hoover Confidential, Anthony Summers, page 13

[179] Vanderbilt Law Review, Volume 43, Issue 3, G. Robert Blakey et Thomas A. Perry, page 985

[180] https://www.nixonfoundation.org/2013/07/the-fight-against-organized-crime-continues/

[181] Criminal Rico: A Manual For Federal Prosecutors, U.S. Department of Justice, page 2

[182] https://www.hbs.edu/faculty/Pages/item.aspx?num=37240

[183] https://supreme.justia.com/cases/federal/us/274/259/

[184] Chicago Sunday Tribune, October 18 1931, page 1

[185] Capone, John Kobler, page 342

[186] Gotti, Jerry Capeci et Gene Mustain, page 176

[187] The American Gladiators: Taft Versus Remus, Albert Rosenberg, page 4

[188] Donnie Brasco: My Undercover Life in the Mafia, Joseph D. Pistone, page 86

[189] Donnie Brasco: My Undercover Life in the Mafia, Joseph D. Pistone, page 96

[190] New York Times, January 16, 1983, page 29

[191] Little Man: Meyer Lansky and the Gangster Life, Robert Lacey, page 4

[192] Little Man: Meyer Lansky and the Gangster Life, Robert Lacey, page 3

[193] Little Man: Meyer Lansky and the Gangster Life, Robert Lacey, page 23

[194] Olives: The Life and Lore of a Noble Fruit, Mort Rosenbaum, page 139

[195] Oncle Frank: Frank Costello, Vie et Mort d'un Parrain, Leonard Katz, page 244

[196] Rothstein: The Life, Times, and Murder of the Criminal Genius Who Fixed the 1919 World Series, David Pietrusza, page 50

[197] Rothstein: The Life, Times, and Murder of the Criminal Genius Who Fixed the 1919 World Series, David Pietrusza, page 224

[198] The Complete Idiot's Guide to the Mafia, Jerry Capeci, appendice B

[199] The Fresno Bee, July 7 1964, page 10

[200] Mafia Princess: Growing Up in Sam Giancana's Family, Antoinette Giancana et Thomas C. Renner, page 90

[201] Mafia Princess: Growing Up in Sam Giancana's Family, Antoinette Giancana et Thomas C. Renner, page 91

[202] Donnie Brasco: My Undercover Life in the Mafia, Joseph D. Pistone, page 267

[203] Donnie Brasco: My Undercover Life in the Mafia, Joseph D. Pistone, page 268

[204] Mr. Capone, Robert J. Schoenberg, page 123

[205] Mr. Capone, Robert J. Schoenberg, page 309

[206] https://www.secretservice.gov/about/history/transportation

[207] https://www.findagrave.com

[208] Mob Boss: The Life of Little Al D'Arco, the Man Who Brought Down the Mafia, Jerry Capeci et Tom Robbins, page 45

[209] Mob Boss: The Life of Little Al D'Arco, the Man Who Brought Down the Mafia, Jerry Capeci et Tom Robbins, page 47

[210] Gotti, Jerry Capeci et Gene Mustain, page 171

[211] Gotti, Jerry Capeci et Gene Mustain, page 176

[212] Mob Boss: The Life of Little Al D'Arco, the Man Who Brought Down the Mafia, Jerry Capeci et Tom Robbins, page 432

[213] We Only Kill Each Other: The Life and Bad Times of Bugsy Siegel, Dean Southern Jennings, page 125

[214] We Only Kill Each Other: The Life and Bad Times of Bugsy Siegel, Dean Southern Jennings, page 159

[215] Oncle Frank: Frank Costello, Vie et Mort d'un Parrain, Leonard Katz, page 244

[216] The Mafia Encyclopedia, Carl Sifakis page 78

[217] The Mafia Encyclopedia, Carl Sifakis, page 174

[218] Rothstein: The Life, Times, and Murder of the Criminal Genius Who Fixed the 1919 World Series, David Pietrusza, page 333

[219] Capone, John Kobler, page 24

[220] Capone, John Kobler, page 27

[221] New York Times, July 16, 1979, page 1

[222] Donnie Brasco: Unfinished Business, Joseph D. Pistone, page 29

[223] Donnie Brasco: Unfinished Business, Joseph D. Pistone, page 30

[224] Homme d'Honneur, Joseph Bonanno, page 8

[225] Capone, John Kobler, page 27

[226] Capone, John Kobler, page 80

[227] Capone, John Kobler, page 128

[228] Rothstein: The Life, Times, and Murder of the Criminal Genius Who Fixed the 1919 World Series, David Pietrusza, page 17

[229] Oncle Frank: Frank Costello, Vie et Mort d'un Parrain, Leonard Katz, page 20

[230] News-Press, Fort Myers, September 24 1945, page 4

[231] Chicago Tribune, July 30, 1993, page 36

[232] The Mafia Encyclopedia, Carl Sifakis page 3

[233] The Mafia Encyclopedia, Carl Sifakis page 304

[234] The Origin of Organized Crime in America: The New York City Mafia, 1891-1931, David Critchley, page 186

[235] https://www.gettyimages.fr/detail/photo-d%27actualit%C3%A9/the-body-of-underworld-kingpin-joe-the-boss-masseria-photo-dactualit%C3%A9/514679792

[236] Uncle Frank: The Biography of Frank Costello, Leonard Katz, page 252

[237] New York Times, May 16, 1998, page 6

[238] https://descendantofthieves.com/

[239] Gotti, Jerry Capeci et Gene Mustain, page 33

[240] Gotti, Jerry Capeci et Gene Mustain, page 225

[241] New York Times, May 16, 1998, page 6

[242] The Mafia Encyclopedia, Carl Sifakis, page 354

[243] Mob Boss: The Life of Little Al D'Arco, the Man Who Brought Down the Mafia, Jerry Capeci et Tom Robbins, page 443

[244] New York Times, December 19, 1997, page 8

[245] Mob Boss: The Life of Little Al D'Arco, the Man Who Brought Down the Mafia, Jerry Capeci et Tom Robbins, page 368

[246] Mob Boss: The Life of Little Al D'Arco, the Man Who Brought Down the Mafia, Jerry Capeci et Tom Robbins, page 369

[247] Mob Boss: The Life of Little Al D'Arco, the Man Who Brought Down the Mafia, Jerry Capeci et Tom Robbins, page 373

[248] Mob Boss: The Life of Little Al D'Arco, the Man Who Brought Down the Mafia, Jerry Capeci et Tom Robbins, page 364

[249] Mob Boss: The Life of Little Al D'Arco, the Man Who Brought Down the Mafia, Jerry Capeci et Tom Robbins, page 374

[250] Mob Boss: The Life of Little Al D'Arco, the Man Who Brought Down the Mafia, Jerry Capeci et Tom Robbins, page 387

[251] New York Times, February 27, 1973, page 78

[252] The Godfather Effect: Changing Hollywood, America, and Me, Tom Santopietro, page 144

[253] Little Man: Meyer Lansky and the Gangster Life, Robert Lacey, page 135

[254] Little Man: Meyer Lansky and the Gangster Life, Robert Lacey, page 137

[255] Little Man: Meyer Lansky and the Gangster Life, Robert Lacey, page 138

[256] Capone: The Man and the Era, Laurence Bergreen, page 511

[257] Capone: The Man and the Era, Laurence Bergreen, page 116

[258] Capone: The Man and the Era, Laurence Bergreen, page 564

[259] Les Secrets de la Mafia, Philippe Di Folco, page 68

[260] Mickey Cohen: The Life and Crimes of L.A.'s Notorious Mobster, Tere Tereba, page 92

[261] Mob Lawyer, Frank Ragano et Selwyn Raab, page 219

[262] https://baseballhall.org/hall-of-famers/brown-mordecai

[263] Homme d'Honneur, Joseph Bonanno, page 169

[264] Homme d'Honneur, Joseph Bonanno, page 285

[265] New York Times, October 16, 1976, page 28

[266] Homme d'Honneur, Joseph Bonanno, page 284

[267] Homme d'Honneur, Joseph Bonanno, page 210

[268] Deal With The Devil: The FBI's Secret Thirty-Year Relationship With a Mafia Killer, Peter Lance, page 189

[269] Deal With The Devil: The FBI's Secret Thirty-Year Relationship With a Mafia Killer, Peter Lance, page 190

[270] Deal With The Devil: The FBI's Secret Thirty-Year Relationship With a Mafia Killer, Peter Lance, page 191

[271] New York Times, August 30, 1992, page 35

[272] Mafia Princess: Growing Up in Sam Giancana's Family, Antoinette Giancana et Thomas C. Renner, page 184

[273] Mafia Princess: Growing Up in Sam Giancana's Family, Antoinette Giancana et Thomas C. Renner, page 183

[274] Mafia Princess: Growing Up in Sam Giancana's Family, Antoinette Giancana et Thomas C. Renner, page 188

[275] Dossier du FBI sur Carmine Galante, fichier NY-92-911, page 14

[276] Five Families: The Rise, Decline, and Resurgence of America's Most Powerful Mafia Empires, Selwyn Raab, page 204

[277] Oncle Frank: Frank Costello, Vie et Mort d'un Parrain, Leonard Katz, page 175

[278] The Last Godfather: The Rise and Fall of Joey Massino, Simon Crittle, page 194

[279] Little Man: Meyer Lansky and the Gangster Life, Robert Lacey, page 70

[280] Little Man: Meyer Lansky and the Gangster Life, Robert Lacey, page 71

[281] Little Man: Meyer Lansky and the Gangster Life, Robert Lacey, page 73

[282] Little Man: Meyer Lansky and the Gangster Life, Robert Lacey, page 437

[283] Little Man: Meyer Lansky and the Gangster Life, Robert Lacey, page 438

[284] Five Families: The Rise, Decline, and Resurgence of America's Most Powerful Mafia Empires, Selwyn Raab, page 56

[285] Five Families: The Rise, Decline, and Resurgence of America's Most Powerful Mafia Empires, Selwyn Raab, page 57

[286] The Mafia at War, Allied Collusion With the Mob, Tim Newark, page 103

[287] The Mafia at War, Allied Collusion With the Mob, Tim Newark, page 112

[288] Smartest Bandit of the Cookson Hills, Carl Janaway, page 117

[289] Brutal: The Untold Story of My Life Inside Whitey Bulger's Irish Mob, Kevin Weeks, page 83

[290] Project MKULTRA, the CIA's Program of Research in Behavioral Modification, U.S. Government, page 69

[291] Brutal: The Untold Story of My Life Inside Whitey Bulger's Irish Mob, Kevin Weeks, page 83

[292] Brutal: The Untold Story of My Life Inside Whitey Bulger's Irish Mob, Kevin Weeks, page 84

[293] Gotti, Jerry Capeci et Gene Mustain, page 439

[294] Iced: The Story of Organized Crime in Canada, Stephen Schneider, page 255

[295] Homme d'Honneur, Joseph Bonanno, page 234

[296] Homme d'Honneur, Joseph Bonanno, page 236

[297] Cigar City Mafia: A Complete History of the Tampa Underworld, Scott Deitche, page 101

[298] Cigar City Mafia: A Complete History of the Tampa Underworld, Scott Deitche, page 99

[299] Cigar City Mafia: A Complete History of the Tampa Underworld, Scott Deitche, page 102

[300] Cigar City Mafia: A Complete History of the Tampa Underworld, Scott Deitche, page 104

[301] Jazz and the Underworld: Dangerous Rhythms, T.J. English, page 291

[302] https://law.justia.com/cases/federal/appellate-courts/F2/352/921/404004/

[303] Mafia Princess: Growing Up in Sam Giancana's Family, Antoinette Giancana et Thomas C. Renner, page 337

[304] The Mafia at War, Allied Collusion With the Mob, Tim Newark, page 69

[305] The Mafia at War, Allied Collusion With the Mob, Tim Newark, page 90

[306] The Mafia at War, Allied Collusion With the Mob, Tim Newark, page 104

[307] The Mafia at War, Allied Collusion With the Mob, Tim Newark, page 91

[308] The Mafia at War, Allied Collusion With the Mob, Tim Newark, page 268

[309] Smartest Bandit of the Cookson Hills, Carl Janaway, page 123

[310] NBC News, April 15, 2006, https://www.nbcnews.com/id/wbna12321039

[311] Les Affranchis: La Vie Quotidienne dans la Mafia, Nicholas Pileggi, page 238

[312] Les Affranchis: La Vie Quotidienne dans la Mafia, Nicholas Pileggi, page 239

[313] Smartest Bandit of the Cookson Hills, Carl Janaway, page 117

[314] The Mad Ones: Crazy Joe Gallo and the Revolution at the Edge of the Underworld, Tom Folsom, page 121

[315] The Mad Ones: Crazy Joe Gallo and the Revolution at the Edge of the Underworld, Tom Folsom, page 131

[316] The Mad Ones: Crazy Joe Gallo and the Revolution at the Edge of the Underworld, Tom Folsom, page 157

[317] Rothstein: The Life, Times, and Murder of the Criminal Genius Who Fixed the 1919 World Series, David Pietrusza, page 30

[318] Rothstein: The Life, Times, and Murder of the Criminal Genius Who Fixed the 1919 World Series, David Pietrusza, page 4

[319] Rothstein: The Life, Times, and Murder of the Criminal Genius Who Fixed the 1919 World Series, David Pietrusza, page 3

[320] Rothstein: The Life, Times, and Murder of the Criminal Genius Who Fixed the 1919 World Series, David Pietrusza, page 10

[321] The Mafia Encyclopedia, Carl Sikakis, page 168

[322] The Mafia Encyclopedia, Carl Sikakis, page 169

[323] Cosa Nostra, un Siècle d'Histoire, Eric Frattini, page 120

[324] We Only Kill Each Other: The Life and Bad Times of Bugsy Siegel, Dean Southern Jennings, page 154

[325] Cosa Nostra, un Siècle d'Histoire, Eric Frattini, page 120

[326] The Mafia Encyclopedia, Carl Sikakis, page 169

[327] Cosa Nostra, un Siècle d'Histoire, Eric Frattini, page 121

[328] We Only Kill Each Other: The Life and Bad Times of Bugsy Siegel, Dean Southern Jennings, page 209

[329] The Sinatra Club: My Life Inside the New York Mafia, Salvatore Polisi, page 3

[330] Golf Chicago Magazine, April 2017, page 19

[331] Mafia, Life Times, page 68

[332] Mr. Capone, Robert J. Schoenberg, page 178

[333] Le Syndicat du Crime, Jean-Michel Charlier, page 219

[334] https://boxrec.com/en/proboxer/59280

[335] Goddess: The Secret Lives of Marilyn Monroe, Anthony Summers, page 270

[336] Oncle Frank: Frank Costello, Vie et Mort d'un Parrain, Leonard Katz, page 93

[337] Oncle Frank: Frank Costello, Vie et Mort d'un Parrain, Leonard Katz, page 102

[338] New York Times, October 14, 1934, page 1

[339] Rothstein: The Life, Times, and Murder of the Criminal Genius Who Fixed the 1919 World Series, David Pietrusza, page 38

[340] Rothstein: The Life, Times, and Murder of the Criminal Genius Who Fixed the 1919 World Series, David Pietrusza, page 40

[341] Little Man: Meyer Lansky and the Gangster Life, Robert Lacey, page 227

[342] Cigar City Mafia: A Complete History of the Tampa Underworld, Scott Deitche, page 98

[343] Little Man: Meyer Lansky and the Gangster Life, Robert Lacey, page 231

[344] Corruption in Cuba: Castro and Beyond, Sergio Díaz-Briquets et Jorge Pérez-López, page 83

[345] Five Families: The Rise, Decline, and Resurgence of America's Most Powerful Mafia Empires, Selwyn Raab, page 104

[346] Raging Bull: My Story, Jack La Motta, Joseph Carter et Peter Savage, page 161

[347] La Mafia à Hollywood, Tim Adler, page 128

[348] Five Families: The Rise, Decline, and Resurgence of America's Most Powerful Mafia Empires, Selwyn Raab, page 312

[349] Fats Waller, Maurice Waller et Anthony Calabrese, page 62

[350] Fats Waller, Maurice Waller et Anthony Calabrese, page 63

[351] Sinatra: The Life, Anthony Summers, page 8

[352] Frank Sinatra, une Mythologie Américaine, Steven Jezo-Vannier, page 21

[353] Frank Sinatra, une Mythologie Américaine, Steven Jezo-Vannier, page 30

[354] Frank Sinatra, une Mythologie Américaine, Steven Jezo-Vannier, page 33

[355] Sinatra: The Life, Anthony Summers, page 21

[356] Mob Boss: The Life of Little Al D'Arco, the Man Who Brought Down the Mafia, Jerry Capeci et Tom Robbins, page 228

[357] https://www.last.fm/music/Anthrax/+wiki

[358] https://www.grammy.com/artists/anthrax/7569

[359] https://www.black-sabbath.com/theband/spitz/

[360] The Bob Dylan Albums: A Critical Study, Anthony Varesi, page 130

[361] The Bob Dylan Albums: A Critical Study, Anthony Varesi, page 132

[362] https://www.bobdylan.com/songs/joey/

[363] https://bestsellingalbums.org/album/5777

[364] Capone: The Man and the Era, Laurence Bergreen, page 81

[365] https://www.imdb.com/title/tt0099674/soundtrack/

[366] https://www.opera-online.com/en/items/works/cavalleria-rusticana-mascagni-targioni-tozzetti-1890

[367] Little Man: Meyer Lansky and the Gangster Life, Robert Lacey, page 148

[368] Little Man: Meyer Lansky and the Gangster Life, Robert Lacey, page 147

[369] Little Man: Meyer Lansky and the Gangster Life, Robert Lacey, page 142

[370] Little Man: Meyer Lansky and the Gangster Life, Robert Lacey, page 149

[371] Frank Sinatra, Steven Jezo-Vannier, page 295

[372] Frank Sinatra, Steven Jezo-Vannier, page 345

[373] Frank Sinatra, Steven Jezo-Vannier, page 246

[374] Frank Sinatra, Steven Jezo-Vannier, page 247

[375] Jazz and the Underworld: Dangerous Rhythms, T.J. English, page 81

[376] Jazz and the Underworld: Dangerous Rhythms, T.J. English, page 82

[377] Jazz and the Underworld: Dangerous Rhythms, T.J. English, page 37

[378] Jazz and the Underworld: Dangerous Rhythms, T.J. English, page 82

[379] Jazz and the Underworld: Dangerous Rhythms, T.J. English, page 96

[380] Jazz and the Underworld: Dangerous Rhythms, T.J. English, page 105

[381] Jazz and the Underworld: Dangerous Rhythms, T.J. English, page 107

[382] Jazz and the Underworld: Dangerous Rhythms, T.J. English, page 108

[383] Jazz and the Underworld: Dangerous Rhythms, T.J. English, page 109

[384] Jazz and the Underworld: Dangerous Rhythms, T.J. English, page 110

[385] Jazz and the Underworld: Dangerous Rhythms, T.J. English, page 111

[386] La Mafia à Hollywood, Tim Adler, page 180

[387] La Mafia à Hollywood, Tim Adler, page 181

[388] La Mafia à Hollywood, Tim Adler, page 182

[389] Frank Sinatra, une Mythologie Américaine, Steven Jezo-Vannier, page 176

[390] Sinatra: The Life, Anthony Summers, page 137

[391] Jazz and the Underworld: Dangerous Rhythms, T.J. English, page 102

[392] On the Rock: Twenty-Five Years in Alcatraz, Alvin Karpis, page 51

[393] On the Rock: Twenty-Five Years in Alcatraz, Alvin Karpis, page 52

[394] Chicago Tribune, April 17 2009, page 1

[395] Jazz and the Underworld: Dangerous Rhythms, T.J. English, page 153

[396] Jazz and the Underworld: Dangerous Rhythms, T.J. English, page 155

[397] https://www.ibdb.com/broadway-production/hot-chocolates-10906

[398] Jazz and the Underworld: Dangerous Rhythms, T.J. English, page 156

[399] Les Secrets de la Mafia, Philippe Di Folco, page 160

[400] Jazz and the Underworld: Dangerous Rhythms, T.J. English, page 203

[401] Five Families: The Rise, Decline, and Resurgence of America's Most Powerful Mafia Empires, Selwyn Raab, page 94

[402] Homme d'Honneur, Joseph Bonanno, page 183

[403] Homme d'Honneur, Joseph Bonanno, page 184

[404] Homme d'Honneur, Joseph Bonanno, page 185

[405] Sinatra: The Life, Anthony Summers, page 341

[406] King of the Godfathers: "Big Joey" Massino and the Fall of the Bonanno Crime Family, Anthony M. Destefano, page 9

[407] King of the Godfathers: "Big Joey" Massino and the Fall of the Bonanno Crime Family, Anthony M. Destefano, page 13

[408] King of the Godfathers: "Big Joey" Massino and the Fall of the Bonanno Crime Family, Anthony M. Destefano, page 18

[409] La Mafia à Hollywood, Tim Adler, page 250

[410] La Mafia à Hollywood, Tim Adler, page 252

[411] https://www.imdb.com/title/tt0068646/

[412] The Godfather Effect: Changing Hollywood, America, and Me, Tom Santopietro, page 74

[413] La Mafia à Hollywood, Tim Adler, page 53

[414] La Mafia à Hollywood, Tim Adler, page 126

[415] La Mafia à Hollywood, Tim Adler, page 91

[416] La Mafia à Hollywood, Tim Adler, page 79

[417] La Mafia à Hollywood, Tim Adler, page 84

[418] La Mafia à Hollywood, Tim Adler, page 89

[419] The Great Gatsby, Francis Scott Fitzgerald, page 78

[420] Rothstein: The Life, Times, and Murder of the Criminal Genius Who Fixed the 1919 World Series, David Pietrusza, page 163

[421] The Great Gatsby, Francis Scott Fitzgerald, page 78

[422] F. Scott Fitzgerald's The Great Gatsby, Matthew Joseph Bruccoli, page 211

[423] Les Secrets de la Mafia, Philippe Di Folco, page 87

[424] Kill the Dutchman!: The Story of Dutch Schultz, Paul Sann, page 334

[425] Kill the Dutchman!: The Story of Dutch Schultz, Paul Sann, page 69

[426] Kill the Dutchman!: The Story of Dutch Schultz, Paul Sann, page 56

[427] Kill the Dutchman!: The Story of Dutch Schultz, Paul Sann, page 57

[428] The Hoffa Wars: The Rise and Fall of Jimmy Hoffa, Dan E. Moldea, page 10

[429] Les Secrets de la Mafia, Philippe Di Folco, page 202

[430] https://www.theguardian.com/film/2022/jul/08/james-caan-obituary

[431] La Mafia à Hollywood, Tim Adler, page 259

[432] We Only Kill Each Other: The Life and Bad Times of Bugsy Siegel, Dean Southern Jennings, page 40

[433] Gangsters and Goodfellas: The Mob, Witness Protection, and Life on the Run, Henry Hill, page 250

[434] Gangsters and Goodfellas: The Mob, Witness Protection, and Life on the Run, Henry Hill, page 249

[435] Le Syndicat du Crime, Jean-Michel Charlier, page 191

[436] Le Syndicat du Crime, Jean-Michel Charlier, page 192

[437] https://www.oscars.org/oscars/ceremonies/1939

[438] Homme d'Honneur, Joseph Bonanno, page 62

[439] Homme d'Honneur, Joseph Bonanno, page 58

[440] Homme d'Honneur, Joseph Bonanno, page 60

[441] https://www.vanityfair.com/hollywood/2012/04/sopranos-oral-history

[442] Five Families: The Rise, Decline, and Resurgence of America's Most Powerful Mafia Empires, Selwyn Raab, page 189

[443] Deal With The Devil: The FBI's Secret Thirty-Year Relationship With a Mafia Killer, Peter Lance, page 91

[444] Five Families: The Rise, Decline, and Resurgence of America's Most Powerful Mafia Empires, Selwyn Raab, page 646

445 https://www.oscars.org/oscars/ceremonies/1944

446 Five Families: The Rise, Decline, and Resurgence of America's Most Powerful Mafia Empires, Selwyn Raab, page 646

447 The United States Attorney's Office, Eastern District of New York, press release April 6, 2006

448 The United States Attorney's Office, Eastern District of New York, press release March 6, 2009

449 https://www.imdb.com/name/nm0258388/

450 Mob Boss: The Life of Little Al D'Arco, the Man Who Brought Down the Mafia, Jerry Capeci et Tom Robbins, page 45

451 The Valachi Papers, Peter Maas, page 129

452 The Evening Times, March 3, 1953, page 2

453 Rothstein: The Life, Times, and Murder of the Criminal Genius Who Fixed the 1919 World Series, David Pietrusza, page 50

454 Jazz and the Underworld: Dangerous Rhythms, T.J. English, page 213

455 Hollywood and the Mob: Movies, Mafia, Sex and Death, Tim Adler, page 176

456 La Mafia à Hollywood, Tim Adler, page 237

457 La Mafia à Hollywood, Tim Adler, page 239

458 La Mafia à Hollywood, Tim Adler, page 122

459 Capone, John Kobler, page 44

460 Capone: The Man and the Era, Laurence Bergreen, page 81

[461] Les Secrets de la Mafia, Philippe Di Folco, page 34

[462] The Encyclopedia of Unsolved Crimes, Michael Newton, page 115

[463] The Mafia Encyclopedia, Carl Sifakis page 414

[464] King of the Godfathers: "Big Joey" Massino and the Fall of the Bonanno Crime Family, Anthony M. Destefano, page 227

[465] Boss of Bosses: The Fall of the Godfather, the FBI and Paul Castellano, Joseph F. O'Brien et Andris Kurins, page 125

[466] Boss of Bosses: The Fall of the Godfather, the FBI and Paul Castellano, Joseph F. O'Brien et Andris Kurins, page 278

[467] Mob Boss: The Life of Little Al D'Arco, the Man Who Brought Down the Mafia, Jerry Capeci et Tom Robbins, page 107

[468] Five Families: The Rise, Decline, and Resurgence of America's Most Powerful Mafia Empires, Selwyn Raab, page 331

[469] New York Daily News, September 29, 1996, page 5

[470] United States District Court, Eastern District of New York, Docket No. 90-CR-446 (S-4) (FB), Seth D. DuCharme, page 3

[471] Mob Boss: The Life of Little Al D'Arco, the Man Who Brought Down the Mafia, Jerry Capeci et Tom Robbins, page 296

[472] The Last Godfather: The Rise and Fall of Joey Massino, Simon Crittle, page 10

[473] The Last Godfather: The Rise and Fall of Joey Massino, Simon Crittle, page 11

[474] The Last Godfather: The Rise and Fall of Joey Massino, Simon Crittle, page 11 of the foreword by Joseph Pistone

[475] Little Man: Meyer Lansky and the Gangster Life, Robert Lacey, page 283

[476] https://www.ncbi.nlm.nih.gov/pmc/articles/PMC2972336/

[477] https://time.com/3665643/deadly-drinking/

[478] https://prohibition.themobmuseum.org/the-history/the-prohibition-underworld/bootleggers-and-bathtub-gin/

[479] Rothstein: The Life, Times, and Murder of the Criminal Genius Who Fixed the 1919 World Series, David Pietrusza, page 3

[480] Boardwalk Empire: The Birth, High Times, and Corruption of Atlantic City, Nelson Johnson, page 91

[481] Boardwalk Empire: The Birth, High Times, and Corruption of Atlantic City, Nelson Johnson, page 92

[482] https://prohibition.themobmuseum.org/the-history/the-prohibition-underworld/the-speakeasies-of-the-1920s/

[483] Mairie de New York, https://www.nyc.gov/assets/mome/pdf/ESI-NYCEDC-Nightlife-Report-2018.pdf

[484] New York Times, May 3, 1972, page 1

[485] The Mafia Encyclopedia, Carl Sifakis page 304

[486] https://www.gettyimages.fr/detail/photo-d%27actualit%C3%A9/the-body-of-underworld-kingpin-joe-the-boss-masseria-photo-dactualit%C3%A9/514679792

[487] Bringing Down the Mob: The War Against the American Mafia, Thomas Reppetto, page 185

[488] The Day, December 17, 1985, page 1

[489] Gotti, Jerry Capeci et Gene Mustain, page 103

[490] Gotti, Jerry Capeci et Gene Mustain, page 110

[491] Cosa Nostra, un Siècle d'Histoire, Eric Frattini, page 91

[492] Cosa Nostra, un Siècle d'Histoire, Eric Frattini, page 92

[493] Mob Boss: The Life of Little Al D'Arco, the Man Who Brought Down the Mafia, Jerry Capeci et Tom Robbins, page 443

[494] The Valachi Papers, Peter Maas, page 197

[495] The New York Times. May 12, 1920. page 2

[496] Mr. Capone, Robert J. Schoenberg, page 61

[497] Five Families: The Rise, Decline, and Resurgence of America's Most Powerful Mafia Empires, Selwyn Raab, page 26

[498] Homme d'Honneur, Joseph Bonanno, page 78

[499] https://prohibition.themobmuseum.org/the-history/the-prohibition-underworld/bootleggers-and-bathtub-gin/

[500] Oncle Frank: Frank Costello, Vie et Mort d'un Parrain, Leonard Katz, page 13

[501] Oncle Frank: Frank Costello, Vie et Mort d'un Parrain, Leonard Katz, page 16

[502] Mafia Princess: Growing Up in Sam Giancana's Family, Antoinette Giancana et Thomas C. Renner, page 69

[503] New York Times, June 21 1975, page 1

[504] Mafia Princess: Growing Up in Sam Giancana's Family, Antoinette Giancana et Thomas C. Renner, page 356

[505] Homme d'Honneur, Joseph Bonanno, page 160

[506] Five Families: The Rise, Decline, and Resurgence of America's Most Powerful Mafia Empires, Selwyn Raab, page 94

[507] Homme d'Honneur, Joseph Bonanno, page 160

[508] The Last Godfather: The Rise and Fall of Joey Massino, Simon Crittle, page 122

[509] The Way of the Wiseguy, Joseph D. Pistone, page 19

[510] Les Secrets de la Mafia, Philippe Di Folco, page 72

[511] Five Families: The Rise, Decline, and Resurgence of America's Most Powerful Mafia Empires, Selwyn Raab, page 565

[512] Five Families: The Rise, Decline, and Resurgence of America's Most Powerful Mafia Empires, Selwyn Raab, page 566